HOW TO
START
A
BUSINESS
IN
MASSACHUSETTS

HOW TO
START
A
BUSINESS
IN
MASSACHUSETTS

Third Edition

Julia K. O'Neill
Mark Warda
Attorneys at Law

 SPHINX® PUBLISHING
AN IMPRINT OF SOURCEBOOKS, INC.®
NAPERVILLE, ILLINOIS
www.SphinxLegal.com

Third Edition, 2003

Sphinx® Publishing, a imprint of Sourcebooks, Inc.®

Naperville Office
P.O. Box 4410
Naperville, Illinois 60567-4410
630-961-3900
Fax: 630-961-2168
www.sourcebooks.com
www.SphinxLegal.com

Interior Design and Production: Amy S. Hall and Edward A. Haman, Sourcebooks, Inc.®

This publication is designed to provide accurate and authoritative information in regard to the subject matter covered. It is sold with the understanding that the publisher is not engaged in rendering legal, accounting, or other professional service. If legal advice or other expert assistance is required, the services of a competent professional person should be sought.

From a Declaration of Principles Jointly Adopted by a Committee of the American Bar Association and a Committee of Publishers and Associations

This product is not a substitute for legal advice.

Disclaimer required by Texas statutes.

Library of Congress Cataloging-in-Publication Data
O'Neill, Julia K.
    How to start a business in Massachusetts / by Julia K. O'Neill and
Mark Warda.-- 3rd ed.
        p. cm.
Includes index.
    ISBN 1-57248-248-6 (pbk.)
  1. New business enterprises--Law and
legislation--Massachusetts--Popular works. I. Warda, Mark. II. Title.
    KFM2552.Z9 O54 2002
    346.744'065--dc21
                                                                2002012181

Printed and bound in the United States of America.
VHG Paperback — 10 9 8 7 6 5 4 3 2 1

CONTENTS

USING SELF-HELP LAW BOOKS

Before using a self-help law book, you should realize the advantages and disadvantages of doing your own legal work and understand the challenges and diligence that this requires.

THE GROWING TREND

Rest assured that you won't be the first or only person handling your own legal matter. For example, in some states, more than seventy-five percent of divorces and other cases have at least one party representing him or herself. Because of the high cost of legal services, this is a major trend and many courts are struggling to make it easier for people to represent themselves. However, some courts are not happy with people who do not use attorneys and refuse to help them in any way. For some, the attitude is, "Go to the law library and figure it out for yourself."

We at Sphinx write and publish self-help law books to give people an alternative to the often complicated and confusing legal books found in most law libraries. We have made the explanations of the law as simple and easy to understand as possible. Of course, unlike an attorney advising an individual client, we cannot cover every conceivable possibility.

COST/VALUE ANALYSIS

Whenever you shop for a product or service, you are faced with various levels of quality and price. In deciding what product or service to buy, you make a cost/value analysis on the basis of your willingness to pay and the quality you desire.

When buying a car, you decide whether you want transportation, comfort, status, or looks. Accordingly, you decide among such choices as a Neon, a Lincoln, a Rolls Royce, or a Porsche. Before making a decision, you usually weigh the merits of each option against the cost.

When you get a headache, you can take a pain reliever or visit a medical specialist for a neurological examination. Given this choice, most people, of course, take a pain reliever, since it costs only pennies; whereas a medical examination costs hundreds of dollars and takes a lot of time. This is usually a logical choice because it is rare to need anything more than a pain reliever for a headache. But in some cases, a headache may indicate a brain tumor and failing to see a specialist right away can result in complications. Should everyone with a headache go to a specialist? Of course not, but people treating their own illnesses must realize that they are betting on the basis of their cost/value analysis of the situation. They are taking the most logical option.

The same cost/value analysis must be made when deciding to do one's own legal work. Many legal situations are very straight forward, requiring a simple form and no complicated analysis. Anyone with a little intelligence and a book of instructions can handle the matter without outside help.

But there is always the chance that complications are involved that only an attorney would notice. To simplify the law into a book like this, several legal cases often must be condensed into a single sentence or paragraph. Otherwise, the book would be several hundred pages long and too complicated for most people. However, this simplification necessarily leaves out many details and nuances that would apply to special or unusual situations. Also, there are many ways to interpret most legal questions. Your case may come before a judge who disagrees with the analysis of our authors.

Therefore, in deciding to use a self-help law book and to do your own legal work, you must realize that you are making a cost/value analysis. You have decided that the money you will save in doing it yourself outweighs the chance that your case will not turn out to your satisfaction. Most people handling their own simple legal matters never have a problem, but occasionally people find that it ended up costing them more to have an attorney straighten out the situation than it would have if they had hired an attorney in the beginning. Keep this in mind if you decide to handle your own case, and be sure to consult an attorney if you feel you might need further guidance.

LOCAL RULES   The next thing to remember is that a book that covers the law for the entire nation, or even for an entire state, cannot possibly include every procedural difference of every county court. Whenever possible, we provide the exact form needed; however, in some areas, each county, or even each judge, may require unique forms and procedures. In our state books, our forms usually cover the majority of counties in the state, or provide examples of the type of form that will be required. In our national books, our forms are sometimes even more general in nature but are designed to give a good idea of the type of form that will be needed in most locations. Nonetheless, keep in mind that your state, county, or judge may have a requirement, or use a form, that is not included in this book.

You should not necessarily expect to be able to get all of the information and resources you need solely from within the pages of this book. This book will serve as your guide, giving you specific information whenever possible and helping you to find out what else you will need to know. This is just like if you decided to build your own backyard deck. You might purchase a book on how to build decks. However, such a book would not include the building codes and permit requirements of every city, town, county, and township in the nation; nor would it include the lumber, nails, saws, hammers, and other materials and tools you would need to actually build the deck. You would use the book as your guide, and then do some work and research involving such matters as whether you need a permit of some kind, what type and grade of wood are available in your area, whether to use hand tools or power tools, and how to use those tools.

Before using the forms in a book like this, you should check with the appropriate authorities to see if there are any local rules of which you should be aware, or local forms you will need to use. Often, such forms will require the same information as the forms in the book but are merely laid out differently, use slightly different language, or use different color paper. They will sometimes require additional information.

CHANGES IN THE LAW

Besides being subject to state and local rules and practices, the law is subject to change at any time. The courts and the legislatures of all fifty states are constantly revising the laws. It is possible that while you are reading this book, some aspect of the law is being changed or a court is interpreting a law in a different way. You should always check the most recent statutes, rules and regulations to see what, if any changes have been made.

In most cases, the change will be of minimal significance. A form will be redesigned, additional information will be required, or a waiting period will be extended. As a result, you might need to revise a form, file an extra form, or wait out a longer time period; these types of changes will not usually affect the outcome of your case. On the other hand, sometimes a major part of the law is changed, the entire law in a particular area is rewritten, or a case that was the basis of a central legal point is overruled. In such instances, your entire ability to pursue your case may be impaired.

Again, you should weigh the value of your case against the cost of an attorney and make a decision as to what you believe is in your best interest.

INTRODUCTION

Each year, thousands of new corporations and limited liability companies are registered in Massachusetts and thousands more partnerships and proprietorships open for business. Entrepreneurship is alive and well in Massachusetts. From restaurants to shopping services or indoor golf courses, the new businesses just keep growing.

The best way to take part in this boom is to run your own business. Be your own boss and be as successful as you dare to be. But if you do not follow the laws of the state, your progress can be slowed or stopped by government fines, civil judgments, or even criminal penalties.

This book is intended to give you the framework for legally opening a business in Massachusetts. It also includes information on where to find special rules for each type of business. If you have problems which are not covered by this book, you should consult an attorney who can be available for your ongoing needs.

In order to cover all of the aspects of any business you are thinking of starting, you should read through this entire book, rather than skipping to the parts which look most interesting. There are many laws which may not sound like they apply to you but which do have provisions which will affect your business.

The forms included in this book were the most recent available at the time of publication. It is possible that some may be revised at the time you read this book. Always check with the secretary of state to be sure you are using the latest forms.

Good luck with your new business!

DECIDING TO START A BUSINESS 1

If you are reading this book, you have probably made a serious decision to take the plunge and start your own business. Hundreds of thousands of people make the same decision each year and many of them become very successful. Some merely eke out a living, others become billionaires, but a lot of them also fail. Knowledge can only help your chances of success. You need to know why some succeed while others fail. Some of what follows may seem obvious, but to someone wrapped up in a new business idea, some of this information is occasionally overlooked.

KNOW YOUR STRENGTHS

The last thing a budding entrepreneur wants to hear is that he is not cut out for running his own business. Those "do you have what it takes" quizzes are ignored with the fear that the answer might be one the entrepreneur does not want to hear. But even if you lack some skills, you can be successful if you know where to get them.

You should consider all of the skills and knowledge necessary to run a successful business and decide whether you have what it takes. If you do not, it doesn't necessarily mean you are doomed to be an employee all your life. Perhaps you just need a partner who has the skills you lack, or perhaps you can hire the skills you need, or can structure your business to avoid areas where you are weak. If those do not work, maybe you can learn the skills.

For example, if you are not good at dealing with employees (either you are too passive and get taken advantage of, or too tough and scare them off), you can:

- handle product development yourself and have a partner or manager deal with employees;

- take seminars in employee management; or,

- structure your business so that you do not need employees. Either use independent contractors or set yourself up as an independent contractor.

Here are some of the factors to consider when planning your business:

- *If it takes months or years before your business turns a profit, do you have the resources to stay afloat?* Businesses have gone under or been sold just before they were about to succeed. Staying power is an important ingredient to success.

- *Are you willing to put in a lot of overtime to make your business a success?* Owners of businesses do not set their own hours, the business sets them for the owner. Many business owners work long hours seven days a week, but they enjoy running their business more than family picnics or fishing.

- *Are you willing to do the dirtiest or most unpleasant work of the business?* Emergencies come up and employees are not always dependable. You might need to mop up a flooded room, spend a weekend stuffing 10,000 envelopes, or work Christmas if someone calls in sick.

- *Do you know enough about the product or service? Are you aware of the trends in the industry and what changes new technology might bring?* Think of the people who started typesetting or printing businesses just before type was replaced by laser printers.

- *Do you know enough about accounting and inventory to manage the business?* Some people naturally know how to save money and do things profitably. Others are in the habit of buying the best and the most expensive of everything. The latter can be fatal to a struggling new business.

- *Are you good at managing employees?* While you can start a business on your own, it is usually difficult to "grow" the business without the help of additional employees. Hiring compatible and competent help is essential to your success.

- *Do you know how to sell your product or service?* You can have the best product on the market, but people are not beating a path to your door. If you are a wholesaler, shelf space in major stores is hard to get, especially for a new company without a record, a large line of products, or a large advertising budget.

- *Do you know enough about getting publicity?* The media receive thousands of press releases and announcements each day and most are thrown away. Do not count on free publicity to put your name in front of the public.

KNOW YOUR BUSINESS

You do not only need to know the concept of a business; you need the experience of working in a business. Maybe you always dreamed of running a bed and breakfast or having your own pizza place, and now that you are laid off you think it is time to use your savings to fulfill your dream. Have you ever worked in such a business? If not, you may have no idea of the day-to-day headaches and problems of the business. For example, do you really know how much to allow for theft, spoilage, and unhappy customers?

You might feel silly taking an entry level job at a pizza place when you would rather start your own, but it might be the most valuable preparation you could have. A few weeks of seeing how a business operates could mean the difference between success and failure.

Working in a business as an employee is one of the best ways to be a success at running such a business. New people with new ideas who work in old stodgy industries have been known to revolutionize them with obvious improvements that no one ever dared to try.

DO THE MATH

Conventional wisdom says you need a business plan before committing yourself to a new venture, but lots of businesses are started successfully without the owner even knowing what a business plan is. They have a great concept, put it on the market, and it takes off. But you at least need to do some basic calculations to see if the business can make a profit. Here are some examples:

- If you want to start a retail shop, determine how many people are close enough to become customers, and how many other stores will be competing for those customers. Visit some of those other shops and see how busy they are. Without giving away your plans to compete, ask some general questions like "how's business?" and maybe they will share their frustrations or successes.

- Whether you sell goods or services, do the math to find out how much profit is in it. For example, if you plan to start a house painting company, find out what you will have to pay to hire painters; what it will cost you for all of the insurance, bonding, and licensing you will need; and what the advertising will cost you. Determine how many jobs you can do per month and what other painters are charging. In some industries in different areas of the country, there may be a large margin of profit or there may be almost no profit.

- Find out if there is a demand for your product or service. Suppose you have designed a beautiful new kind of candle and your friends all say you should open a shop because "everyone will want them." Before making a hundred of them and renting a store, bring a few to craft shows or flea markets and see what happens.

●   Calculate what the income and expenses would be for a typical month of your new business. List monthly expenses such as rent, salaries, utilities, insurance, taxes, supplies, advertising, services, and other overhead. Then figure out how much profit you will average from each sale. It is important to estimate how many sales you will need to cover your overhead and divide that number by the number of business days in the month. Can you reasonably expect that many sales? How will you get those sales?

Most types of businesses have trade associations, which often have figures on how profitable its members are. Some even have "start-up" kits for people wanting to open businesses. One good source of information on such organizations is the *Encyclopedia of Associations* published by Gale Research Inc. It is available in many library reference sections. Producers of products to the trade often give assistance to small companies getting started to win their loyalty. Contact the largest suppliers of the products your business will be using and see if they can be of help.

SOURCES OF FURTHER GUIDANCE

The following offices offer free or low cost guidance for new businesses:

Small Business Administration. Provides information on starting, financing, and expanding a business. Call 617-565-5590 or visit their website at: **www.sba.gov/regions/states/ma**.

National Association for the Self-Employed. A 300,000-member group of small-business owners tracking legislative activities, stimulating and encouraging grass-roots businesses, and providing members with educational opportunities and health benefits. Call 800-232-6273 or visit their website at: **www.nase.org**.

Business Resource Center. Provides information for small businesses on getting started, marketing, management, financing, etc. Visit their website at: **www.morebusiness.com**.

SCORE ***Service Corps of Retired Executives.*** Retired business executives volunteer their time to share their management and technical expertise with present and prospective owners and managers of small businesses.

Boston	617-565-5591	Worcester	508-753-2929
Cape Cod	508-775-4884	Springfield	413-785-0314
Brockton	508-587-2673	New Bedford	508-994-5093
	Northeastern Mass.	978-922-9441	

Visit their website at **www.sba.gov/regions/states/ma/score.html**.

MASSACHUSETTS DEVELOPMENT CENTERS ***Massachusetts Department of Economic Development.*** The Department of Economic Development is a state agency responsible for job creation and economic development in Massachusetts. Call 617-727-8380 or visit their website: **www.massconnect.state.ma.us**.

Massachusetts Office of Business Development. The office of Business Development is a division of the Department of Economic Development. This office provides financial, technical, informational, and various other types of assistance to businesses in Massachusetts. Call 1-800-5-CAPITAL or 617-973-8600, or visit their website at **www.massconnect.state.ma.us/showpage.asp?file=dept/mobdoverview.htm**. They have loads of information online. You can also call the regional offices listed below.

Greater Boston Region:	617-973-8686
Central Region (Worcester):	508-792-7506
Northeast Region (Lowell):	978-970-1193
Southeast Region (Dartmouth):	508-997-1438
Western Region (Springfield):	413-784-1580

SOMWBA

The State Office of Minority and Women's Business Assistance. SOMWBA is located within the Massachusetts Department of Economic Development. This agency promotes the development of certified minority business enterprises, women-owned business enterprises, and minority non-profit and women's non-profit organizations. Call 617-973-8692 or visit their website at **www.somwba.state.ma.us**.

CORPORATION
DEVELOPMENT

The Commonwealth Corporation. The Commonwealth Corporation is a government-sponsored entity that provides services to business owners and employees to promote economic growth in Massachusetts. Call 617-727-8158 or visit their website: **www.commcorp.org**.

SMALL BUSINESS
DEVELOPMENT
CENTERS

Massachusetts Technology Development Corporation. The Technology Development Corporation provides funding for start-up and expansion of early-stage technology companies operating in Massachusetts. Call 617-723-4920 or visit their website: **www.mtdc.com**.

Massachusetts Small Business Development Centers. Small Business Development Centers stem from a program sponsored by a consortium of colleges and universities, providing management, technical assistance counseling, and educational programs to small businesses.

State Office: 413-545-6301

Counseling Centers:

Clark University SBDC:	508-793-7615
U Mass Dartmouth SBDC:	508-673-9783
Boston College SBDC:	617-552-4091
Salem State College SBDC:	978-542-6343
Western Mass. Regional Office:	413-737-6712
U Mass Boston SBDC and Minority Business Assistance Center:	617-287-7750
Export Center:	617-973-8664

Or, visit their website: **msbdc.som.umass.edu**

Massachusetts Alliance for Economic Development. The Massachusetts Alliance for Economic Development is a private, non-profit corporation dedicated to fostering economic growth in Massachusetts. It provides free, customized information relating to facility relocation and expansion. Call 617-247-7800 or visit their website: **www.massecon.com**.

Boston Entrepreneurs' Network. The Boston Entrepreneurs' Network provides resources for starting and building businesses. Call 617-325-9852 or visit their website: **www.boston-enet.org**.

Worcester Area Chamber of Commerce. The Worcester Area Chamber of Commerce is the largest Chamber of Commerce in New England. It provides many networking opportunities and more. Call 508-753-2924 or visit their website: **www.worcesterchamber.org**.

Cambridge Business Development Center. The Business Development Center in Cambridge provides resources and support for emerging businesses, including counseling, referrals, and sponsored events. Call 617-349-4690 or visit their website: **www.cbdc.org**.

Foundation for Continuing Education. The Foundation for Continuing Education is a non-profit educational resource that presents seminars and publishes books in the areas of finance, estate and business planning, taxes, business development, and computer programming. Call 978-468-6528 or visit their website: **www.fce.org**.

The Enterprise Center at Salem State College. The Enterprise Center is a mixed-use business park with space available to established and start-up companies. On-site support services, business incubator program and an entrepreneurs' network to help new and emerging businesses on the North Shore. Call 978-542-7528 or visit their website: **www.enterprisectr.org**.

Choosing the Form of Your Business

2

Basic Forms of Business

The six most common forms of business entities in Massachusetts are proprietorship, partnership, corporation, limited partnership, limited liability company, and limited liability partnership. Some of the characteristics, advantages, and disadvantages of each are as follows:

PROPRIETORSHIP

Characteristics. A *proprietorship* is one person doing business in his or her own name *or* under a *fictitious name*.

Advantages. Simplicity is just one advantage. There is also no organizational expense, and no extra tax forms or reports.

Disadvantages. The proprietor is personally liable for all debts and obligations. Also, there is no continuation of the business after death. All profits are directly taxable, certainly a disadvantage for the proprietor, and business affairs are too easily mixed with personal affairs.

GENERAL PARTNERSHIP

Characteristics. A *general partnership* involves two or more people carrying on a business together and sharing the profits and losses.

Advantages. Partners can combine expertise and assets. A general partnership allows liability to be spread among more persons. Also, the business can be continued after the death of a partner if bought out by the surviving partner.

Disadvantages. Each partner is liable for acts of other partners within the scope of the business. This means that if your partner harms a customer or signs a million-dollar credit line in the partnership name, you can be personally liable. All profits are taxable, even if left in the business.

NOTE: *Two more disadvantages: control is shared by all parties and the death of a partner may result in liquidation. In a general partnership, it is often hard to get rid of a bad partner.*

CORPORATION

Characteristics. A *corporation* is an artificial legal "person" that carries on business through its officers and directors, for its shareholders. (In Massachusetts, one person may form a corporation and be the sole shareholder, director, and officer.) Laws covering most business corporations are contained in Massachusetts General Laws, Chapter 156B. The corporation, which is a legal "person," carries on business in its own name and shareholders are usually not liable for its acts.

In a corporation, the *shareholders* elect the directors, and the directors elect the officers. In Massachusetts, if the corporation has three or fewer shareholders, it must have at least the same number of directors. The officers have authority to run the day-to-day operations, but they need directors' approval to do anything out of the ordinary, such as sign a lease for business space, hire an executive employee, or start a new line of business. For even more major decisions such as sale of all or substantially all of the assets of the corporation, merger, reorganization, consolidation or amendment to the articles of organization, a shareholders' vote is required.

An *amendment* to the ARTICLES OF ORGANIZATION is required in order to increase the number of authorized shares of stock, add another class or series of stock, change the corporation's name and to take various other actions. In Massachusetts a majority shareholder vote is required to authorize some amendments to the articles of organization, including a change of the corporation's name or a stock split, but for more major matters such as merger or consolidation, or sale of all or substantially all of the assets, a two-thirds vote is required, unless the company's articles of organization provide for a lesser vote.

Types. An *S corporation* is a corporation which has filed IRS Form 2553 choosing to have all profits taxed to, and other tax attributes flow through to, the shareholders rather than to the corporation. An S corporation files a tax return but pays no federal tax. The profits (or losses) shown on the S corporation tax return are reported on the owners' tax returns. In Massachusetts, even an S corporation must pay the minimum state excise tax of $456 per year.

Generally, to elect S corporation status, the following conditions must be satisfied:

- the corporation must be a U.S. corporation;

- there must be no more than seventy-five shareholders;

- shareholders may only be individuals, estates, specified types of trusts, or certain exempt organizations; and,

- only one class of stock is allowed, although the voting rights can differ.

A C *corporation* is any business corporation that has not elected to be taxed as an S corporation. A C corporation pays both state and federal income tax on its profits. The effect of having business profits taxed at the corporate level, unlike the S corporation, is that the profits are taxed twice: once at the corporate level (as income to the corporation) and a second time at the shareholder level (as dividend income to the shareholder).

A *professional corporation* is a corporation formed by a professional such as a doctor or accountant. Massachusetts has special rules for professional corporations which differ slightly from those of other corporations. These rules are included in Chapter 156A of the Massachusetts General Laws. A professional corporation may be an S corporation.

Massachusetts laws require a majority of the directors and all of the officers other than treasurer, clerk, assistant treasurer and assistant clerk of a professional corporation to be a licensed practitioners of the profession that the corporation has been organized to practice. When filing the organizational documents, the incorporators of a professional corporation have to obtain proof from the appropriate licensing board that the necessary persons are duly licensed.

In addition, Massachusetts law prohibits the issuance or transfer of shares to a person who is not professionally licensed. The various licensing boards also often have authority, by statute, to promulgate additional requirements with which professional corporations must comply.

A *nonprofit corporation* is usually used for organizations such as churches and condominium associations. However, with careful planning, some types of businesses can be set up as nonprofit corporations and save a fortune in taxes. While a nonprofit corporation cannot pay dividends, it can pay its officers and employees fair salaries. Some of the major American nonprofit organizations pay their officers well over $100,000 a year. Massachusetts' special rules for nonprofit corporations are included in Chapter 180 of the Massachusetts General Laws.

Advantages. If a corporation is properly organized and maintained, shareholders have no liability for corporate debts and lawsuits. Also, officers and directors usually have no personal liability for their corporate acts. The existence of a corporation may be perpetual, that is, it will survive changes in owners. There are tax advantages allowed only to corporations; and there is prestige in owning a corporation. Two excellent advantages: capital may be raised by issuing stock, and it is fairly easy to transfer ownership upon death. A small corporation can be set up as an S corporation to avoid corporate taxes but still retain corporate advantages, such as limited liability. Some types of businesses can be set up as nonprofit corporations which provide significant tax savings.

Disadvantages. There are start-up costs for forming a corporation; plus there are certain formalities such as annual meetings, separate bank accounts, and special tax forms. Unless a corporation registers as an S corporation, it must pay federal income tax separate from the tax paid by the owners, and may pay more than the minimum state excise tax.

LIMITED
PARTNERSHIP

Characteristics. A *limited partnership* has characteristics similar to both a corporation and a partnership. There are *general partners* who have the control and personal liability, and there are *limited partners* who only put up money and whose liability is limited to what they paid for their share of the partnership (like corporate stock).

Advantages. *Capital* can be contributed by limited partners who have no control of the business or liability for its debts.

Disadvantages. A great disadvantage is high start-up costs. Also, an extensive partnership agreement is required because general partners are personally liable for partnership debts and for the acts of each other. (One solution to this problem is to use a corporation as the general partner.)

LIMITED
LIABILITY
COMPANY

Characteristics. Massachusetts was one of the last states to allow the formation of a limited liability company. As an alternative to the corporate form, the LLC is steadily gaining in popularity. This entity is like a limited partnership without general partners. It has characteristics of both a corporation and a partnership. None of the members have liability and all can have some control, and it does not have to be taxed for federal purposes at the company level but can choose to be taxed like a partnership.

Advantages. The limited liability company offers the tax benefits of a partnership (if the entity chooses to be taxed as a partnership rather than a corporation) with the protection from liability of a corporation. It offers more tax benefits and flexibility than an S corporation because it may pass through more depreciation and deductions. Allocations of income, gain, loss, deduction, and credit can be made in proportions which are different than the equity owners' respective ownership interests, subject to various limitations.

It may have different classes of ownership, an unlimited number of members, and aliens as members. If it owns appreciated property, it has more favorable tax treatment upon dissolution than an S corporation. The limited liability company is also extremely flexible in structure and operational aspects, since those are not dictated strictly by statute as they are for corporations.

Disadvantages. There are higher start-up costs than for a corporation. Due to the flexibility in structural and operational aspects, the governing documents are more complex and expensive to have properly prepared than those of a corporation. Since Massachusetts does not yet allow one-person LLCs, the death of a co-member can cause dissolution of the entity. The LLC may also be subject to personal property tax on inventory in Massachusetts to which a corporation would not be subject.

LIMITED
LIABILITY
PARTNERSHIP

Characteristics. The limited liability partnership is like a general partnership, but without personal liability. It was devised to allow partnerships of lawyers and other professionals limit their personal liability without losing their partnership structure.

NOTE: *The law does not allow professionals to limit their liability for negligence in their own professional functions, i.e., malpractice.*

This was important because converting to an LLC could have tax consequences, and some states do not allow professionals to operate as LLCs. Both general and limited partnerships can register as LLPs. In Massachusetts, lawyers cannot practice in an LLC entity; therefore, they often use the limited liability partnership.

Advantages. The LLP offers the flexibility and tax benefits of a partnership with the protection from liability of a corporation.

Disadvantages. Start-up and annual fees are higher for limited liability partnerships than for a corporation.

MASSACHUSETTS S-CORPORATIONS VERSUS MASSACHUSETTS LLCS

Often the start-up will narrow down its choices of entity to two—the S corporation and the LLC. Both entities will protect the principals from any personal liability for the business's debts and obligations, assuming formalities are followed and no circumstances lend themselves to a creditor's being able to *pierce the corporate veil*. Both entities also have their income taxed to the principals on a pass-through basis, such that there is no tax at the entity level, but only at the individual owner level. However, the S corporation must pay an annual minimum excise tax of $456 to the Commonwealth of Massachusetts. If an S corporation's annual receipts exceed six million dollars, the entity could become liable for substantial state income taxes. The LLC is not liable for any state excise tax.

Different circumstances may point to a choice of one type of entity or another. There are always pros and cons to both choices. But being aware of the differences and similarities between these two types of entities will help you to make the right choice.

FILING FEES   The cost of the annual filing fee for the LLC, however, makes up for the lack of excise tax liability. The fee for filing an LLCs annual report with the secretary of state is $500, while the S corporation's annual filing fee is $125. The initial filing fees for forming the entities are $500 for an LLC and $275 (minimum, depending on the amount of stock authorized) for the S corporation. Thus, while the initial fees differ by $225, the annual fees for upkeep for the two types of entities are substantially similar.

RESTRICTIONS ON TRANSFER   Both the LLC and the S corporation lend themselves easily to restrictions on transfer to protect the principals from having outsiders as co-owners. The LLCs operating agreement can include these restrictions on transfer and buy-sell provisions. The shares in an S corporation can be made subject to such provisions by their inclusion in the ARTICLES OF ORGANIZATION or by contract.

Some practitioners and business people assume that "newer is better." They automatically choose the LLC over the S corporation because the LLC is new and more modern and therefore, must be better. As when you choose a computer or a word-processing program, you should evaluate how you plan to use it, what you plan to do with it in the future, and other various implications of the choice in order to select the model that is right for you.

STATUTES The structure and functioning of the S corporation are governed by statute, as described earlier. The laws do not allow for variation on most of the rules by the entity or its owners. The LLC, however, is much more flexible. The statutes allow for a great deal of leeway in selecting the method of governance of the entity. If the owners wish, they can make one person a manager with all the authority in the world (almost). An LLC does not have to have any officers or directors. The entity can be set up, operated and terminated any number of ways. There is a myriad of choices available to persons forming an LLC.

Although flexibility can be a bonus, it carries with it a certain level of complexity which some people would rather avoid. The flexibility that comes with an LLC necessarily involves decision-making which some may find daunting.

In making this decision, you should also consider whether your business is likely to ever go public. If so, an LLC will not work. The business could, however, convert from an LLC to a corporation prior to going public, with not too much trouble or tax consequence (see below).

OWNERS/ Another major difference between the LLC and the S corporation
MEMBERS relates to the number and type of owners or members. Massachusetts does not yet allow one-member LLCs (a change in this regard may be forthcoming), but there are no other restrictions on how many members an LLC may have or who they may be—e.g., individuals, corporations, or other entities. The S corporation may have as few as one shareholder but no more than seventy-five (husband and wife are treated as one), and they must meet certain criteria. They must be individuals, estates, certain types of trusts or certain exempt organizations, and they may not be nonresident aliens. The S corporation can only have one class of stock (although differences solely in voting rights are allowed). The LLC can have many different types of owners and equity interests in one entity.

Currently one of the major drawbacks of the Massachusetts LLC is that it must begin with at least two members. The death or withdrawal of all but one of an LLC's members can cause the automatic termination of the entity and thus a removal of the limited liability shield (often without the knowledge of the people involved). If there are only a few principals in the business, this could be a major consideration.

TAXES   Although the tax treatment of the two types of entities is generally similar (i.e., tax attributes flow through to the equity owner level, and there is no entity-level tax), there are some differences which should be considered.

One tax aspect to consider is that the income of an LLC that flows through to persons involved with the business will generally be subject to self-employment tax. With an S corporation, only salaries are subject to self-employment tax. If other income is paid out as S corporation distributions, it will not be subject to self-employment tax.

NOTE: *In this regard that the IRS has broad authority to characterize income as it sees fit.*

A second tax difference between the two entities is that in an LLC, distributions of appreciated property will generally be tax free, and the members will have a carry over basis in the distributed assets. Not so with an S corporation. Distributed appreciated assets will cause shareholders in an S corporation to have taxable income and take a basis of current fair market value in the assets. This is the major reason that conversion from an S corporation to an LLC creates tax issues, while conversion from an LLC to an S corporation generally does not.

A third, and major, tax difference is that in the LLC, generally owners can have different allocations of tax benefits like depreciation and losses, without regard to their pro rata ownership interests. The S corporation cannot make special allocations of these tax items.

There can be a major tax problem for Massachusetts LLCs which are in a business that carries inventory. The personal property tax statutes specifically exempt personal property of domestic business corporations, but not of LLCs. This means that an LLC with substantial personal property (e.g., inventory such as automobiles) will be liable for property tax which the business would not have been liable for had it been formed as a corporation. This legislative omission could be a costly trap for some businesses.

The LLC is generally preferable to the S corporation where the entity will own real estate subject to substantial debt, because the LLC provides the benefit of member-level tax basis adjustments for LLC liabilities and the allowance of an adjustment in the tax basis of the entity's assets upon the sale of a member's interest. The S corporation shareholder cannot include any part of the corporation's debt in the tax basis of his stock, unless he loaned the money to the corporation. Because of these differences, LLC members are able to deduct more of the entity's tax losses as they occur than S corporation shareholders.

Start-up Procedures

For those entities which are required to make filings with the secretary of state, the Corporations Division's website has loads of information and forms. It is located at **www.state.ma.us/sec/cor/coridx.htm**.

PROPRIETORSHIP
In a proprietorship, all accounts, property, and licenses are taken in the name of the owner. (See Chapter 3 for using a fictitious name.)

PARTNERSHIP
To form a partnership, a written agreement should be prepared to spell out rights and obligations of the parties. (See Chapter 3 for using a fictitious name.) Most accounts, property and licenses can be in either the partnership name or that of the partners.

CORPORATION
To form a corporation, **Articles of Incorporation** must be filed with the Secretary of State in Boston, along with a minimum filing fee of $275. An organizational meeting is then held at which officers are elected, stock issued, and other formalities observed. If these formalities are not followed, you risk the possibility of a creditor being able to "pierce the corporate veil," or have the corporate entity set aside in order to render shareholders personally liable for the company's obligations. Contracts, licenses, accounts, and the like are in the name of the corporation.

LIMITED PARTNERSHIP   A **CERTIFICATE OF LIMITED PARTNERSHIP** must be drawn up and registered with the Secretary of State in Boston, and generally, a lengthy disclosure document must be given to all prospective limited partners. Because of the complexity of securities laws and the criminal penalties for violation, it is advantageous to have an attorney organize a limited partnership.

LIMITED LIABILITY COMPANY   Two or more persons may form a limited liability company by filing **ARTICLES OF ORGANIZATION** with the Secretary of State in Boston. The filing fee is $500. Contracts, licenses, and accounts are in the name of the company.

LIMITED LIABILITY PARTNERSHIP   Two or more persons may form a limited liability partnership by filing a registration form with the Secretary of State in Boston. The filing fee is $500. Licenses and accounts are in the name of the company.

Required Contacts

TYPES OF BUSINESS	AGENCY	DIVISION	TELEPHONE	REQUIREMENT	FREQUENCY
Business Corporation	Secretary of Commonwealth	Corporations	(617)727-9640	• file Articles of Organization • file Articles of Amendment • file Annual Report • file Articles of Dissolution	Once When Necessary Annually Upon termination
Professional Corporation	Secretary of Commonwealth	Corporations	(617)727-9640	• same as for business corporation, plus; -a certificate of the appropriate regulating board(s) that each of the incorporators, the president, and any vice presidents, a majority of the directors and each shareholder is duly licensed, must accompany Articles of Organization.	Once
Non-Profit Corporation	Secretary of Commonwealth	Corporations	(617) 727-9640	• same as for business corporations except: -file Annual Report -dissolved through court action	Annually on November 1
Foreign Corporation	Secretary of Commonwealth	Corporations	(617) 727-9640	• file Certificate of Registration • file amended certificate • file Annual Report • file Certificate of Withdrawal	Once When necessary Annually Upon cessation of business in the Commonwealth
Limited Partnership	Secretary of the Commonwealth	Corporations	(617) 727-2859	• file Certificate of Limited Partnership • file amended certificate • file Certificate of Cancellation	Once When necessary Upon dissolution
Foreign Limited Partnership	Secretary of the Commonwealth	Corporations	(617) 727-2859	• file Certificate of Registration • file amended certificate • file Certificate of Withdrawal	Once When necessary Upon cessation of business in the Commonwealth Upon dissolution
Business Trust	Secretary of the Commonwealth	Corporations	(617) 727-2859	• file Declaration of trust • file amended declaration • file Annual Report	Once When Necessary Annually
	Secretary of the Commonwealth	Securities Division	(617) 727-3548 1-800-269-5428	• broker/dealer registration • investment advisor registration • corporate finance section	When necessary When necessary When necessary

TYPE OF BUSINESS	AGENCY	DIVISION	TELEPHONE	REQUIREMENT	FREQUENCY
Limited Liability Companies	Secretary of the Commonwealth	Corporations	(617) 727-2859	Domestic: • file Certificate of Organization • file Certificate of Amendment • file Annual Report • file Certificate of Cancellation Foreign: • file Registration • file Amendment • file Annual Report • file Certificate of Withdrawal	Once When necessary Annually Upon dissolution Once When necessary Annually Upon dissolution
Limited Liability Partnerships	Secretary of the Commonwealth	Corporations	(617) 727-2859	Domestic and Foreign: • file Certificate of Registration • file Amendment Registration • file Annual Report • file Certificate of Withdrawal	Once When necessary Annually Upon withdrawal of registration or dissolution

Business Comparison Chart

	Sole Proprietorship	General Partnership	Limited Partnership	Limited Liability Co.	Limited Liability Partnership	Corporation C or S	Nonprofit Corporation
Liability Protection	No	No	For limited partners	For all members	For all members	For all shareholders	For all members
Taxes	Pass through	Pass through	Pass through	Pass through	Pass through	S corps. pass through; C corps. pay tax	None
Minimum # of members	1	2	2	2	2	1	1
Start-up fee	None	None	$200	$500	$500	Min $275	35
Annual fee	None	None	N/A	$500	$500	$125	$15
Diff. classes of ownership	No	No	Yes	Yes	Yes	S corps. No C corps. Yes	No ownership Diff. classes of membership
Survives after Death	No	No	Yes	Yes unless fewer than 2 members remain	No	Yes	Yes
Best for	1 person low-risk business or no assets	low-risk business	low-risk business with silent partners	All types of businesses	Law Firms	All types of businesses	Educational

BUSINESS START-UP CHECKLIST

- ❏ Make your plan
    - ❏ Obtain and read all relevant publications on your type of business
    - ❏ Obtain and read all laws and regulations affecting your business
    - ❏ Calculate whether your plan will produce a profit
    - ❏ Plan your sources of capital
    - ❏ Plan your sources of goods or services
    - ❏ Plan your marketing efforts
- ❏ Choose your business name
    - ❏ Check other business names and trademarks
    - ❏ Register your name, trademark, etc.
- ❏ Choose the business form
    - ❏ Prepare and file organizational papers
    - ❏ Prepare and file fictitious name if necessary
- ❏ Choose the location
    - ❏ Check competitors
    - ❏ Check zoning
- ❏ Obtain necessary licenses
    - ❏ City?   ❏ State?
    - ❏ County?   ❏ Federal?
- ❏ Choose a bank
    - ❏ Checking
    - ❏ Credit card processing
    - ❏ Loans
- ❏ Obtain necessary insurance
    - ❏ Worker's Comp   ❏ Automobile
    - ❏ Unemployment   ❏ Liability
    - ❏ Health   ❏ Hazard
    - ❏ Life/disability
- ❏ File necessary federal tax registrations
- ❏ File necessary state tax registrations
- ❏ Set up a bookkeeping system
- ❏ Plan your hiring
    - ❏ Obtain required posters
    - ❏ Obtain or prepare employment application
    - ❏ Obtain new hire tax forms
    - ❏ Prepare employment policies
    - ❏ Determine compliance with health and safety laws
- ❏ Plan your opening
    - ❏ Obtain all necessary equipment and supplies
    - ❏ Obtain all necessary inventory
    - ❏ Do all necessary marketing and publicity
    - ❏ Obtain all necessary forms and agreements
    - ❏ Prepare your company policies on refunds, exchanges, returns

YOUR BUSINESS NAME 3

PRELIMINARY CONSIDERATIONS

Before deciding upon a name for your business, you should be sure that it is not already being used by someone else. Many business owners have spent thousands of dollars on publicity and printing, only to throw it all away because another company owned the name. A company that owns a name can take you to court and force you to stop using that name. It can also sue you for damages if it thinks your use of the name caused it a financial loss.

If you will be running a small local shop with no plans for expansion, you should at least check out whether the name has been trademarked. If someone else is using the same name anywhere in the country and has registered it as a federal trademark, they can sue you. If you plan to expand or to deal nationally, you should do a more thorough search of the name.

The first places to look are the local phone books and city or town clerk's office (for a fictitious name filing). Next, you should check with the Secretary of State's office in Boston to see if someone has registered a corporate or LLC name which is the same as, or confusingly similar to, the one you have chosen. The secretary of state's office can be reached at 617-727-2850 or 617-727-9640.

To do a national search, you should check trade directories and phone books of major cities. These can be found at many libraries, but are usually reference books which can only be used at the library. The *Trade Names Directory* is a two volume set of names compiled from many sources and published by Gale Research Company. If you have a computer with Internet access, you can use it to search the yellow pages at **www.yellowpages.com**.

To be sure that your use of the name does not violate someone else's trademark rights, you should have a trademark search done in the United States Patent and Trademark Office (USPTO). In the past, this required a visit to their offices or the hiring of a search for over a hundred dollars. The USPTO put its trademark records online in 1999 and you can now search them at: **http://tess.uspto.gov**. Keep in mind that this database is not kept altogether current. If you do not have access to the Internet, you might be able to do it on a computer at a public library or have one of their employees order an online search for a small fee. If this is not available to you, you can have the search done through a firm, such as Thomson & Thomson at **www.thomson-thomson.com** or 800-692-8833.

No matter how thorough your search, there is no guarantee that there is not a local user somewhere with rights to the mark. If, for example, you register a name for a new chain of restaurants and later find out that someone in Tucumcari, New Mexico, has been using the name longer than you, that person will still have the right to use the name but probably just in his local area. If you do not want his restaurant to cause confusion with your chain, you can offer to buy it. Similarly, if you are operating a small business under a unique name and a law firm in New York writes and offers to buy the right to your name, you can assume that some large corporation wants to start a major expansion under that name.

The best way to make sure a name you are using is not already owned by someone else is to make up a name. Names such as Xerox, Kodak, and Exxon were made up and did not have any meaning prior to their use. Remember that there are millions of businesses, so even something you make up may already be in use. Do a search anyway.

FICTITIOUS NAMES

In Massachusetts, as in most states, unless you do business in your own legal name, you must register the business name (called a *fictitious name*) you are using. The name must be registered with the clerk of each city and town where you have an office.

A fictitious name registration is good for four years and can be renewed for additional four-year periods. Failure to make the required filings can result in fines of $300 per month.

If your name is Jennifer Anne and you are operating a fan store, you may operate your business as "Jennifer Anne, Portable Fans" without registering it. But variations on your name, such as "Jenny Anne, the Fan Fan," should be registered.

You cannot use the words "corporation," "incorporated," "corp.," or "inc.," unless you are a corporation. However, a corporation does not have to register the name it is using unless it is different from its registered corporate name. A partnership does not have to register the name it is using as long as it contains the surname of any partner.

Legally, when you use a fictitious name, you are "doing business as" (d/b/a) whatever name you are using; e.g., "Jennifer Anne d/b/a Jenny Anne, The Fan Fan."

As discussed above, you should do some research to see if the name you intend to use is already being used by anyone else. Even persons who have not registered a name can acquire legal rights to the name through use.

At the end of this chapter is a sample fictitious name form for the city of Boston. Most cities and towns have their own form. You should call the city or town clerk and ask them to send you their form. If they do not have one, you can use the generic form in the appendix.

CORPORATE NAMES

A corporation does not have to register a fictitious name unless it uses a name which is different from its true legal name. In the judgment of the secretary of state, the name of a corporation must include a word or words indicating that it is a corporation. Regulations indicate that one of the following words will suffice:

Incorporated	Inc.
Corporation	Corp.
Limited	Ltd.

The word "company" or "co." is not sufficient.

If the name of the corporation does not contain one of the above words, it will probably be rejected by the secretary of state. It will also be rejected if the name used by it is already taken or is similar to the name of another corporation, or if it uses a forbidden word such as "Bank" or "Trust." To check on a name, you may call the secretary of state at 617-727-2850.

If a name you choose is taken by another company, you may be able to change it slightly and have it accepted. For example, if there is already a Fisher Cut Bait, Inc., in a different county, you may be allowed to use Fisher Cut Bait, Inc. of Dukes County. But even if approved by the secretary of state, you may get sued by the other company if your business is close to theirs, or there is a likelihood of confusion.

Also, do not have anything printed until your corporate papers are returned to you. Sometimes a name is approved over the phone and rejected when submitted.

Once you have chosen a corporate name and know it is available, you should immediately form your corporation. A name can be "reserved" for a month for $15, but it is easier just to form the corporation than to waste time on the name reservation.

If a corporation wants to do business under a name other than its corporate name, it can register a fictitious name such as "Luke the Duke of Earl, Inc., d/b/a Luke the Duke." However, if the name used leads people to believe that the business is not a corporation, there may be some risk of losing the right to limited liability that the corporate entity provides. If such a name is used, it should always be accompanied by the corporate name.

PROFESSIONAL CORPORATIONS

Professional corporations are corporations formed by professionals such as attorneys, doctors, dentists, and architects. In Massachusetts, a professional corporation can use any of the usual corporate designations, Inc., Corp., and so on, or the words "Professional Corporation" or the abbreviation "P.C."

THE WORD "LIMITED"

The words *Limited* or *Ltd.* at the end of a name can be used for a corporation, although some people find this confusing because they associate the word with a limited partnership. The *Limited Liability Company* is a new form of doing business which was just recently authorized in Massachusetts. The phrase "Limited Liability Company," or its abbreviation, "L.L.C.," should only be used with such an entity.

DOMAIN NAMES

A discussion of domain names is contained in Chapter 15 of this book.

TRADEMARKS

As your business builds goodwill, its name will become more valuable and you will want to protect it from others who may wish to copy it. To protect a name used to describe your goods or services, you can register it as a trademark (for goods) or a service mark (for services) with either the Secretary of State of Massachusetts or with the United States Patent and Trademark Office.

You cannot register a trademark for the name of your business unless that name is also the name of goods or services you are selling. In many cases, you use your company name on your goods as your trademark. In effect, it protects your company name. Another way to protect your company name is to incorporate. A particular corporate name can only be registered by one company in Massachusetts.

STATE
REGISTRATION

State registration would be useful if you only expect to use your trademark within Massachusetts. Federal registration would protect your mark anywhere in the country. Use of a mark without registration does give you some legal rights to the mark, but registration of the mark gives you much better protection. The registration of a mark constitutes proof that you are the exclusive owner of the mark for the types of goods or services for which you register it. The only exception is persons who have already been using the mark. People who have been using the mark prior to your registration may have superior rights even though they have not registered the mark.

The procedure for state registration is simple and the cost is $50. First, you should write to the Secretary of State, Trademark Division, One Ashburton Place, Boston, MA 02108 or call 617-727-2859 to ask them to search your name and tell you if it is available. For questions about filing the application, call the same number.

Before a mark can be registered, it must be used in Massachusetts. For goods, this means it must be used on the goods themselves, or on containers, tags, labels, or displays of the goods. For services, it must be used in the sale or advertising of the services. The use must be in an actual transaction with a customer. A sample mailed to a friend is not considered acceptable use.

The $50 fee will register the mark in only one "class of goods." If the mark is used on more than one class of goods, a separate registration must be filed. Three "specimens" of use of the mark must also be filed. The registration is good for ten years. It must be renewed six months prior to its expiration. The renewal fee is $50 for each class of goods.

At the end of this chapter is the MASSACHUSETTS CLASSIFICATION OF GOODS AND SERVICES (similar, but not identical to, the federal classifications).

FEDERAL REGISTRATION

The procedure for federal registration is a little more complicated. There are two types of applications depending upon whether you have already made actual use of the mark or whether you merely have an intention to use the mark in the future. For a trademark which has been in use, you must file an application form along with specimens showing actual use and a drawing of the mark that complies with all of the rules of the United States Patent and Trademark Office. For an *intent to use* application, you must file two separate forms: one when you make the initial application, and the other after you have made actual use of the mark as well as the specimens and drawing. Before a mark can be entitled to federal registration, the use of the mark must be in *interstate commerce* or in commerce with another country. The fee for registration is $325; but if you file an *intent to use* application, there is a second fee of $100 for the filing after actual use.

Massachusetts classification of goods are as follows:

1. Chemical products used in industry, science, photography, agriculture, horticulture, forestry; artificial and synthetic resins; plastics in the form of powders, liquids or pastes, for industrial use; manures (natural and artificial); fire extinguishing compositions; tempering substances and chemical preparations for soldering; chemical substances for preserving foodstuffs; tanning substances; adhesive substance used in industry.

2. Paints, varnishes, lacquers, preservatives against rust and against deterioration of wood; coloring matters, dyestuffs; mordants; natural resins; metals in foil and powder form for painters and decorators.

3. Bleaching preparations and other substances for laundry use; cleaning, polishing, scouring and abrasive preparations; soaps; perfumery; essential oils, cosmetics, hair lotions; dentifrices.

4. Industrial oils and greases (other than edible oils and fats and essential oils); lubricants; dust laying and absorbing compositions; fuels (including motor spirit) and illuminants; candles, tapers, nightlights and wicks.

5. Pharmaceutical veterinary and sanitary substances; infants' and invalids' food; plasters, material for bandaging; material for stopping teeth, dental wax; disinfectants; preparations for killing weeds and destroying vermin.

6. Unwrought and partly wrought common metals and their alloys; anchors, anvils, bells, rolled and cast building materials; rails and other metallic materials for railway tracks; chains (except driving chains for vehicles); cables and wires (nonelectric); locksmiths' work; metallic pipes and tubes; safes and cash boxes; steel balls; horseshoes; nails and screws other goods in non-precious metal included in other classes; ores.

7. Machines and machine tools; motors (except for land vehicles); machine couplings and belting (except for land vehicles); large size agricultural implements; incubators.

8. Hand tools and instruments; cutlery, forks and spoons; side arms.

9. Scientific, nautical, surveying and electrical apparatus and instruments (including wireless), photographic, cinematographic, optical, weighing, measuring, signalling, checking (supervision), lifesaving and teaching apparatus and instruments; coin or counter-freed apparatus; talking machines; cash registers; calculating machines; fire-extinguishing apparatus.

10. Surgical, medical, dental and veterinary instruments and apparatus (including artificial limbs, eyes, and teeth).

11. Installations for lighting, heating, steam generating, cooking, refrigerating, drying, ventilating, water supply and sanitary purposes.

12. Vehicles; apparatus for locomotion by land, air, or water.

13. Firearms; ammunition and projectiles; explosive substances; fireworks.

14. Precious metals and their alloys and goods in precious metals or coated therewith (except cutlery, forks, and spoons); jewelry, precious stones, horological and other chronometric instruments.

15. Musical instruments (other than talking machines and wireless apparatus).

16. Paper and paper articles, cardboard and cardboard articles; printed matter, newspapers and periodicals, books; binding material, photographs; stationery, adhesive materials (stationery); artists' materials; paint brushes; typewriters and office requisites (other than furniture); instructional and teaching material (other than apparatus); playing cards; printers' type and cliches (stereotype).

17. Cutta percha, india rubber, balata and substitutes, articles made from these substances and not included in other classes; plastics in the form of sheets, blocks and rods, being for use in manufacture; materials for packing, stopping or insulating; asbestos, mica and their products; hose pipes (nonmetallic).

18. Leather and imitations of leather, and articles made from these materials and not included in other classes; skins, hides; trunks and travelling bags; umbrellas, parasols and walking sticks; whips, harness and saddlery.

19. Building materials, natural and artificial stone, cement, lime, mortar, plaster and gravel; pipes of earthenware or cement; road making materials; asphalt, pitch and bitumen; portable buildings; stone monuments; chimney pots.

20. Furniture, mirrors, picture frames; articles (not included in other classes) of wood, cork, reeds, cane, wicker, horn, bone, ivory, whalebone, shell, amber, mother-of-pearl, meerschaum, celluloid, substitutes for all these materials, or of plastics.

21. Small domestic utensils and containers (not of precious metal or coated therewith); combs and sponges; brushes (other than paint brushes); brush-making materials; instruments and material for cleaning purposes; steelwool; glassware, porcelain and earthenware, not included in other classes.

22. Ropes, string, nets, tents, awnings, tarpaulins, sails, sacks; padding and stuffing materials (hair, kapok, feathers, seaweed, etc.); raw fibrous textile materials.

23. Yarns, threads.

24. Fabrics (piece goods); bed and table covers; textile articles not included in other classes.

25. Clothing, including boots, shoes and slippers.

26. Lace and embroidery, ribbons and braids; buttons, press buttons, hooks and eyes, pins and needles; artificial flowers.

27. Carpets, rugs, mats and matting; linoleum and other materials for covering floors; wall hangings (non-textile).

28. Games and playthings; gymnastics and sporting articles (except clothing); ornaments and decorations for Christmas trees.

29. Meat, fish, poultry and game; meat extracts; preserved, dried and cooked fruits and vegetables; jellies, jams, eggs, milk and other dairy products; edible oils and fats; preserves, pickles.

30. Coffee, tea, cocoa, sugar, rice, tapioca, sago, coffee substitutes; flour, and preparations made from cereals; breads, biscuits, cakes, pastry and confectionary, ices; honey, treacle; yeast, baking-powder; salt, mustard; pepper, vinegar, sauces, spices; ice.

31. Agricultural, horticultural and forestry products and grains not included in other classes; living animals; fresh fruits and vegetables; seeds; live plants and flowers; foodstuffs for animals, malt.

32. Beer, ale and porter; mineral and aerated waters and other nonalcoholic drinks; syrups and other preparations for making beverages.

33. Wine, spirits and liqueurs.

34. Tobacco, raw or manufactured; smokers' articles; matches.

Classification of services are:

35. Advertising and business.

36. Insurance and financial.

37. Construction and repair.

38. Communication.

39. Transportation and storage.

40. Material treatment.

41. Education and entertainment.

42. Miscellaneous.

FINANCING YOUR BUSINESS **4**

The way to finance your business is determined by how fast you want your business to grow and how much risk of failure you are able to handle. Letting the business grow with its own income is the slowest but safest way to grow. Taking out a personal loan against your house to expand quickly is one of the fastest but riskiest ways to grow.

GROWING WITH PROFITS

Many successful businesses have started out with little money and used the profits to grow bigger and bigger. If you have another source of income to live on (such as a job or a spouse), you can plow all the income of your fledgling business into growth.

Some businesses start as hobbies or part time ventures on the weekend while the entrepreneur holds down a full time job. Many types of goods or service businesses can start this way. Even some multi-million dollar corporations, such as Apple Computer, started out this way.

This allows you to test your idea with little risk. If you find you are not good at running that type of business, or the time or location was not right for your idea, all you have lost is the time you spent and your start-up capital.

However, a business can only grow so big from its own income. In many cases, as a business grows, it gets to a point where the orders are so big that money must be borrowed to produce the product to fill them. With this kind of order, there is the risk that if the customer cannot pay or goes bankrupt, the business will also fail. At such a point, a business owner should investigate the credit-worthiness of the customer and weigh the risks. Some businesses have grown rapidly, some have gone under, and others have decided not to take the risk and stayed small. You can worry about that down the road.

USING YOUR SAVINGS

If you have savings you can tap to get your business started, that is the best source. You will not have to pay high interest rates and you won't have to worry about paying anyone back.

HOME EQUITY

If you have owned your home for several years, it is possible that the equity has grown substantially and you can get a second mortgage to finance your business. If you have been in the home for many years and have a good record of paying your bills, some lenders will make second mortgages that exceed the equity. Just remember, if your business fails, you may lose your house.

RETIREMENT ACCOUNTS

Be careful about borrowing from your retirement savings. There are tax penalties for borrowing from or against certain types of retirement accounts. Also, your future financial security may be lost if your business does not succeed.

HAVING TOO MUCH MONEY

It probably does not seem possible to have too much money with which to start a business, but many businesses have failed for that reason. With plenty of start-up capital available, a business owner does not need to watch expenses and can become wasteful. Employees get used to lavish spending. Once the money runs out and the business must run on its own earnings, it fails.

Starting with the bare minimum forces a business to watch its expenses and be frugal. It necessitates finding the least expensive solutions to problems that crop up and creative ways to be productive.

BORROWING MONEY

It is extremely tempting to look to others to get the money to start a business. The risk of failure may be less worrisome and the pressure may be lower, but that is a problem with borrowing. You may not have the same incentive to succeed if you are using someone else's money as you would if everything you own is on the line.

Actually, you should be even more concerned when using the money of others. Your reputation should be more valuable than the money itself which can always be replaced. Yet, that is not always the case. How many people borrow again and again from their parents for failed business ventures?

FAMILY   Depending on how much money your family can spare and the status of your relationship, borrowing from family members may be the most comfortable or most uncomfortable source of funds for you. If you have been assured a large inheritance and your parents have more funds than they need to live on, you may be able to borrow against your inheritance without worry. It will be your money anyway and you need it much more now than you will ten, twenty, or more years from now. If you lose it all, it is your own loss anyway.

However, if you are borrowing your widowed mother's source of income, asking her to cash in a CD she lives on to finance your get-rich-quick scheme, you should have second thoughts about it. Stop and consider all the real reasons your business might not take off and what your mother would do without the income.

FRIENDS   Borrowing from friends is like borrowing from family members. If you know they have the funds available and could survive a loss, you may want to risk it, but if they would be loaning you their only resources, do not chance it.

Financial problems can be the worst thing for a relationship, whether it is a casual friendship or a long term romantic involvement. Before you borrow from a friend, try to imagine what would happen if you could not pay it back and how you would feel if it caused the end of your relationship.

The ideal situation is if your friend were a co-venturer in your business and the burden would not be totally on you to see how the funds were spent. Still, realize that such a venture will put extra strain on the relationship.

BANKS
In a way, a bank can be a more comfortable party from which to borrow because you do not have a personal relationship with the bank as you do with a friend or family member. If you fail, they will write your loan off rather than disown you. However, a bank can also be the least comfortable party to borrow from because it will demand realistic projections and be on top of you to perform. If you do not meet the bank's expectations, it may call your loan just when you need it most.

The best thing about a bank loan is that they will require you to do your homework: you must have plans that make sense to a banker. If they approve your loan, you know that your plans are at least reasonable.

Bank loans are not cheap or easy. You will be paying a good interest rate, and you will have to put up collateral. If your business does not have equipment or receivables, the bank may require you to put up your house and other personal property to guarantee the loan.

Banks are a little easier to deal with when you get a *Small Business Administration* (SBA) loan. That is because the SBA guarantees that it will pay the bank if you default on the loan. SBA loans are obtained through local bank branches.

CREDIT CARDS
Borrowing against a credit card is one of the fastest growing ways of financing a business, but it can be one of the most expensive ways. The rates can go higher than twenty percent, but many cards offer lower rates and some people are able to get numerous cards. Some successful businesses have used the partners' credit cards to get off the ground or

to weather through a cash crunch, but if the business does not begin to generate the cash to make the payments, you could soon end up in bankruptcy. A good strategy is only to use credit cards for a long term asset like a computer or for something that will quickly generate cash, like buying inventory to fill an order. Do not use credit cards to pay expenses that are not generating revenue.

A Rich Partner

One of the best business combinations is a young entrepreneur with ideas and ambition and a retired investor with business experience and money. Together, they can supply everything the business needs.

How to find such a partner? Be creative. You should have investigated the business you are starting and know others who have been in such businesses. Have any of them had partners retire over the last few years? Are any of them planning to phase out of the business?

Selling Ownership Interests in Your Business

Silent investors are the best source of capital for your business. You retain full control of the business and if it happens to fail you have no obligation to them. Unfortunately, few silent investors are interested in a new business. It is only after you have proven your concept to be successful and built up a rather large enterprise, that you will be able to attract such investors.

The most common way to obtain money from investors is to issue other types of stock or ownership interests to them. The best types of business entities for this are the corporation and the limited liability company. There is almost unlimited flexibility in the number and kinds of ownership interests you can issue.

BUY-SELL AGREEMENTS

If you do sell ownership interests in your business to outsiders, and even if you have co-owners that are involved in the business with you, you should make sure to have arrangements in place that govern what happens to those ownership interests of the owner dies, tries to voluntarily sell his interest, becomes disabled, or otherwise leaves the business (for those owners that are involved in the business). Disaster can strike when ownership interests pass to heirs or other transferees that you never contemplated having as business partners. You can also protect yourself by providing yourself and your heirs with a way to "cash out" in the event that you die or become disabled. These arrangements are usually contained in a "buy-sell" agreement, in a corporation's "shareholders'" agreement, and in the operating agreement of a limited liability company. They are complex and involve differing tax consequences. You should consult an attorney to get the proper arrangements in place.

SECURITIES LAWS

There is one major problem with selling stock in your business and that is all of the federal and state regulations with which you must comply. Both the state and federal governments have long and complicated laws dealing with the sales of "securities." There are also hundreds of court cases attempting to explain what these laws mean. A thorough explanation of this area of law is obviously beyond the scope of this book.

Basically, securities have been held to exist in any case in which a person provides money to someone with the expectation that he will get a profit through the efforts of that person. This can apply to any situation where someone buys stock or other ownership interest in, or makes a loan to, your business. What the laws require is disclosure of the risks involved and other material information, and in some cases, registration of the securities with the government. There are some exemptions, such as for small amounts of money and for limited numbers of investors.

Penalties for violation of securities laws are severe, including triple damages and prison terms. You should consult a specialist in securities laws before issuing any security. You can often get an introductory consultation at a reasonable rate to learn your options.

USING THE INTERNET TO FIND CAPITAL

The owners of Wit Beer made headlines in all the business magazines in 1995 by successfully raising $1.6 million for their business on the Internet. It seemed so easy, every business wanted to try. What was not made clear in most of the stories was that the owner was a corporate securities lawyer and that he did all of the necessary legal work to prepare a prospectus and properly register the stock, something which would have cost anyone else over $100,000 in legal fees. Also, most of the interest in the stock came from the articles, not from the Internet promotion. Today, a similar effort would probably not be nearly as successful.

Before attempting to market your company's shares on the Internet, be sure to get an opinion from a securities lawyer or do some serious research into securities laws.

The Internet does have some sources of capital listed. The following sites may be helpful:

America's Business Funding Directory:
www.businessfinance.com

Angel Capital Electronic Network:
https://ace-net.sr.unh.edu/pub

Small Business Administration:
www.sba.gov

FinanceHub:
www.financehub.com

NVST:
www.nvst.com

Inc. Magazine:
http://mothra.inc.com/finance

The Capital Network:
www.thecapitalnetwork.com

LOCATING YOUR BUSINESS 5

The right location for your business will be determined by what type of business it is, and how fast you expect to grow. For some types of businesses, the location will not be important to your success or failure; but in others, it will be crucial.

WORKING OUT OF YOUR HOME

Many small businesses get started out of the home. Chapter 6 discusses the *legalities* of home businesses. This section discusses the *practicalities*.

Starting a business out of your home can save you the rent, electricity, insurance, and other costs of setting up at another location. For some people this is ideal, and they can combine their home and work duties easily and efficiently, but for other people it is a disaster. A spouse, children, neighbors, television, and household chores can be so distracting that no other work gets done.

Since residential rates are usually lower than business lines, many people use their residential telephone line to conduct business or add a second residential line. However, if you wish to be listed in the yellow pages, you will need to have a business line in your home. If you are running two or more types of businesses, you can probably add their names as additional listings on the original number and avoid paying for another business line.

You also should consider whether the type of business you are starting is compatible with a home office. For example, if your business mostly consists of making phone calls or calling clients, the home may be an ideal place to run it. The home may not be a good location if your clients need to visit you or you will need daily pickups and deliveries by truck. This is discussed in more detail in the next chapter.

CHOOSING A RETAIL SITE

For most types of retail stores, the location is of prime importance. Such things to consider are how close it is to your potential customers, how visible it is to the public, and how easily accessible it is to both autos and pedestrians. The attractiveness and safety should also be considered.

Location would be less important for a business which was the only one of its kind in the area. For example, if there was only one moped parts dealer or Armenian restaurant in a metropolitan area, people would have to come to wherever you are if they want your products or services. However, even with such businesses, keep in mind that there is competition. People who want moped parts can order them by mail and restaurant customers can choose another type of cuisine.

You should look up all the businesses like the one you plan in the phone book and mark them on a map. For some businesses, like a cleaners, you would want to be far from the others. But for other businesses, like antique stores, you would want to be near the others. Since antique stores usually do not carry the same things, they do not compete and people like to go to an "antique district" and visit all the shops.

Choosing an Office, Manufacturing, or Warehouse Space

If your business will be the type where customers will not come to you, locating it near customers is not as much of a concern and you can probably save money by locating away from the high traffic, central business districts. However, you should consider the convenience for employees and not locate in an area which would be unattractive to them, or too far from where they would likely live.

For manufacturing or warehouse operations, you should consider your proximity to a post office, trucking company, or rail line. Where several sites are available, you might consider which one has the earliest or most convenient pick-up schedule for the carriers you plan to use.

Leasing a Site

A lease of space can be one of the biggest expenses of a small business, so you should do a lot of homework before signing one. There are a lot of terms in a commercial lease which can make or break your business. The following are the most critical.

Zoning

Before signing a lease, you should be sure that everything that your business will need to do is allowed by the zoning of the property.

Restrictions

In some shopping centers, existing tenants have guarantees that other tenants do not compete with them. For example, if you plan to open a restaurant and bakery, you may be forbidden to sell carry-out baked goods if the supermarket has a bakery and a noncompete clause.

Signs

Business signs are regulated by zoning laws, sign laws, and property restrictions. If you rent a hidden location with no possibility for adequate signage, your business will have a lot smaller chance of success than with a more visible site or much larger sign.

ADA
COMPLIANCE

The *Americans with Disabilities Act* (ADA) requires that reasonable accommodations be made to make businesses accessible to the handicapped. When a business is remodeled many more changes are required than if no remodeling is done. When renting space, you should be sure that it complies with the law, that the landlord will be responsible for compliance, or that you are aware of the full costs you will bear.

EXPANSION

As your business grows, you may need to expand your space. The time to find out about your options is before you sign the lease. Perhaps you you can take over adjoining units when those leases expire.

RENEWAL

Location is a key to success for some businesses. If you spend five years building up a clientele, you do not want someone to take over your locale at the end of your lease. Therefore, you should have a renewal clause on your lease. This usually allows an increase in rent based on inflation.

GUARANTEE

Most landlords of commercial space will not rent to a small corporation without a personal guaranty of the lease. This is a very risky thing for a new business owner to do. The lifetime rent on a long term commercial lease can be hundreds of thousands of dollars and if your business fails, the last thing you want to do is be personally responsible for several years of rent.

Where space is scarce or a location is hot, a landlord can get the guarantees he demands and there is nothing you can do about it (except perhaps set up an asset protection plan ahead of time). But where several units are vacant or the commercial rental market is soft, you can often negotiate out of the personal guaranty. If the lease is five years, maybe you can get away with a guaranty of just the first year. Give it a try.

DUTY TO OPEN

Some shopping centers have rules requiring all shops to be open certain hours. If you cannot afford to staff it the whole time required or if you have religious or other reasons which make this a problem, you should negotiate it out of the lease or find another location.

SUBLEASE   At some point you may decide to sell your business, and in many cases, the location is the most valuable aspect of it. For this reason you should be sure that you have the right to either *assign* your lease or to *sublease* the property. If this is impossible, one way around a prohibition is to incorporate your business before signing the lease and then when you sell the business, sell the stock. But some lease clauses prohibit transfer of "any interest" in the business, so read the lease carefully.

BUYING A SITE

If you are experienced with owning rental property, you will probably be more inclined to buy a site for your business. If you have no experience with real estate, you should probably rent and not take on the extra cost and responsibility of property ownership.

One reason to buy your site is that you can build up equity. Rather than pay rent to a landlord you can pay off a mortgage and eventually own the property.

SEPARATING THE OWNERSHIP   One risk in buying a business site is that if the business gets into financial trouble the creditors may go after the building as well. For this reason most people who buy a site for their business keep the ownership out of the business. For example, the business will be a corporation and the real estate will be owned personally by the owner or by a trust unrelated to the business.

EXPANSION   Before buying a site, you should consider the growth potential of your business. If it grows quickly will you be able to expand at that site or will you have to move? Might the property next door be available for sale in the future if you need it? Can you get an option on it?

If the site is a good investment whether or not you have your business then by all means buy it. But if its main use is for your business, think twice.

ZONING   When you buy a site, you might be faced with the some of the same concerns you would have if you were renting. You will want to make sure that the zoning permits the type of business you wish to start, or that you can get a variance without a large expense or delay. Be aware that just because a business is now using the site does not mean that you can expand or remodel the business at that site. Some zoning laws allow businesses to be grandfathered in, but not expanded. Check with the zoning department and find out exactly what is allowed.

SIGNS   Signs are another concern. Some cities have regulated signs and do not allow new ones, or require them to be smaller. Some businesses have used these laws to get publicity. A car dealer who was told to take down a large number of American flags on his lot filed a federal lawsuit and rallied the community behind him. It could not have hurt business except for a few over-controlling public officials.

ADA COMPLIANCE   ADA compliance is another concern when buying a commercial building. Find out from the building department if the building is in compliance or what needs to be done to put it in compliance. If you remodel, the requirements may be more strict.

NOTE: *When dealing with public officials, keep in mind that they do not always know what the law is, or do not accurately explain it. They often try to intimidate people into doing things that are not required by law. Read the requirements yourself and question the officials if they seem to be interpreting it wrong. Seek legal advice if officials refuse to reexamine the law, or move away from an erroneous position.*

NOTE: *Also consider that keeping them happy may be worth the price. If you are already doing something they have overlooked, do not make a big deal over a little thing they want changed, or they may subject you to a full inspection or audit.*

CHECK GOVERNMENTAL REGULATIONS

When looking for a site for your business, you should investigate the different governmental regulations in your area. For example, a location just outside the city or county limits might have a lower licensing fee, a lower sales tax rate, and less strict signage requirements.

LICENSING YOUR BUSINESS

OCCUPATIONAL LICENSES AND ZONING

Some Massachusetts cities require you to obtain an occupational license. If you are in a city, you may need both a city and a state license. Businesses which do work in several cities sometimes must obtain a license from each city in which they do work.

City licenses are usually available at city hall. Be sure to find out if zoning allows your type of business before buying or leasing property. The licensing departments will check the zoning before issuing your license.

If you will be preparing or serving food, you will need to check with the local health department to be sure that the premises are in compliance with their regulations.

HOME BUSINESSES

Problems occasionally arise when persons attempt to start a business in their home. Small new businesses cannot afford to pay rent for commercial space and cities often try to forbid business in residential areas. Getting an occupational license or advertising a fictitious name often gives notice to the city that a business is being conducted in a residential area.

Some people avoid the problem by starting their businesses without obtaining the necessary licenses or fictitious name filings, figuring that the penalties for not having done so (if they are caught) are less expensive than the cost of office space. Some also avoid zoning restrictions. If a person regularly parks commercial trucks and equipment on his property, or has delivery trucks coming and going, or employee cars parked along the street, there will probably be complaints from neighbors and the city will probably take legal action. But if a person's business consists merely of making phone calls out of the home and keeping supplies there, the problem may never become an issue.

If a problem does arise regarding a home business which does not disturb the neighbors, a good argument can be made that the zoning law which prohibits the business is unconstitutional. When zoning laws were first instituted, they were not meant to stop people from doing things in a residence which had historically been part of the life in a residence. Consider an artist. Should a zoning law prohibit a person from sitting in his home and painting pictures? If he sells them for a living is there a difference? Can the government force him to rent commercial space just because he decides to sell the paintings he paints?

Similar arguments can be made for many home businesses. For hundreds of years people performed income-producing activities in their homes. (The authors are waiting for their city fathers to tell them to stop writing books in their home offices.) But court battles with a city are expensive and probably not worth the effort for a small business. The best course of action is to keep a low profile. Using a post office box for the business is sometimes helpful in diverting attention away from the residence.

STATE REGULATED PROFESSIONS

The state requires licensing of certain professions and occupations. If you are in a regulated profession, you should be aware of the laws which apply to your profession. The following pages contain a list of many of these professions and the state laws covering them. You can make copies of these laws and related regulations at any law library. You can also find these laws on the Internet at:

www.state.ma.us./legis/laws/mgl/index.htm

If you do not think your profession is regulated, you should read through the list anyway. Some of those included may surprise you.

Regulated Professions in Massachusetts
and the Statutes Governing Them
Citations are to Massachusetts General Laws (M.G.L.)

If no Sections are specified, the entire chapter cited applies.

	M.G.L. Chapter	Section(s)
Attorneys	221	37-52
Physicians and Surgeons	112	2-9B
Physicians Assistants	112	9C-9K
Podiatrists	112	13-22
Athletic Trainers and Occupational/Physical Therapists	112	23A-23Q
Respiratory Therapists	112	23R-23BB
Pharmacists	112	24-36
Sellers of Drugs	112	36A-42A
Dentists	112	43-53
Veterinarians	112	54-60
Architects	112	60A-60O
Optometrists	112	66-73B
Dispensing Opticians	112	73C-73M
Nurses	112	74-81C
Professional Engineers and Land Surveyors	112	81D-81T
Embalmers and Funeral Directors	112	82-87
Certified Public Accountants	112	87A-87E 1/2
Barbers	112	87F-87S

Cosmetologists	112	87T-87KK
Sanitarians	112	87LL-87OO
Real Estate Brokers and Salesmen	112	87PP-87DDD 1/2
Electrologists	112	87EEE-87OOO
Radio and Television Technicians	112	87PPP-87VVV
Certified Health Officers	112	87WWW-87ZZZ
Drinking Water Supply Facility Operators	112	87CCCC-87DDDD
Chiropractors	112	89-97
Landscape Architects	112	98-107
Nursing Home Administrators	112	108-117
Psychologists	112	118-129A
Social Workers	112	130-137
Speech-Language Pathologists and Audiologists	112	138-147
Acupuncturists	112	148-162
Allied Mental Health and Human Services Professionals	112	163-172
Real Estate Appraisers	112	173-195
Certain Mortgage Brokers and Lenders	255E	
Auctioneers	100	
Labeling, Distribution, Sale, Storage, Transportation, Use and Disposal of Pesticides	132B	
Financing Motor Vehicles	255B	

FEDERAL LICENSES

So far, there are few businesses that require federal registration. If you are in any of the types of businesses listed below, you should check with the federal agency listed below it.

Radio or television stations or manufacturers of equipment emitting radio waves:

> Federal Communications Commission
> 1919 M Street, NW
> Washington, DC 20550
> www.fcc.gov

Manufacturers of alcohol, tobacco or firearms:

> Bureau of Alcohol, Tobacco and Firearms,
> Treasury Department
> 1200 Pennsylvania Ave., NW
> Washington, DC 20226
> www.atf.treas.gov

Securities brokers and providers of investment advice:

> Securities and Exchange Commission
> 450 5th Street NW
> Washington, DC 20549
> www.sec.gov

Manufacturers of drugs and processors of meat:

> Food and Drug Administration
> 5600 Fishers Lane
> Rockville, MD 28057
> www.fda.gov

Interstate carriers:

> Surface Transportation Board
> 12th St. & Constitution Ave.
> Washington, DC 20423
> www.stb.dot.gov

Exporting:

> Bureau of Export Administration
> Department of Commerce
> 14th St. & Constitution Ave., NW
> Washington, DC 20220
> www.bxa.doc.gov

Contract Laws 7

As a business owner, you will need to know the basics of forming a simple contract for your transactions with both customers and vendors. There is a lot of misunderstanding about what the law is and people may give you erroneous information. Relying on it can cost you money. This chapter will give you a quick overview of the principles which apply to your transactions and the pitfalls to avoid. If you face more complicated contract questions, you should consult a law library or an attorney familiar with small business law.

Traditional Contract Law

One of the first things taught in law school is that a *contract* is not legal unless three elements are present: offer, acceptance, and consideration. The rest of the semester in contracts class the students dissect exactly what may be a valid offer, acceptance, and consideration. For your purposes, the important things to remember are:

- if you make an offer to someone, it may result in a binding contract, even if you change your mind or find out it was a bad deal for you;

- unless an offer is accepted and both parties agree to the same terms, there is no contract;

- a contract does not always have to be in writing. Some laws require certain contracts to be in writing, but as a general rule an oral contract is legal. The problem is proving that the contract existed; and,

- without consideration (the exchange of something of value or mutual promises), there is not a valid contract.

As mentioned above, an entire semester is spent analyzing each of the three elements of a contract. The most important rules for the business owner are:

- An advertisement is not an offer. Suppose you put an ad in the newspaper offering "New IBM computers only $1995!" but there is a typo in the ad and it says $19.95? Can people come in and say "I accept, here's my $19.95," thereby creating a legal contract? Fortunately, no. Courts have ruled that the ad is not an offer which a person can accept. It is an invitation to come in and make offers, which the business can accept or reject.

- The same rule applies to the price tag on an item. If someone switches price tags on your merchandise, or if you accidentally put the wrong price on it, you are not required by law to sell it at that price. If you intentionally put the wrong price, you may be liable under the "bait and switch" law. And many merchants honor a mistaken price just because refusing to would constitute bad will and probably lose a customer.

- When a person makes an offer, several things may happen. It may be accepted, creating a legal contract. It may be rejected. It may expire before it has been accepted. Or, it may be withdrawn before acceptance. A contract may expire either by a date made in the offer ("This offer remains open until noon on January 29, 2005") or after a reasonable amount of time. What is reasonable is a legal question which a court must decide. If someone makes you an offer to sell goods, clearly you cannot come back five years later and accept. Can you accept a week later or a month later and create a legal contract? That depends on the type of goods and the circumstances.

- A person accepting an offer cannot add any terms to it. If you offer to sell a car for $1,000, and the other party says they accept as long as you put new tires on it, there is no contract. An acceptance with changed terms is considered a rejection and a counteroffer.

- When someone rejects your offer and makes a counteroffer, a contract can be created by your acceptance of the counteroffer.

These rules can affect your business on a daily basis. Suppose you offer to sell something to one customer over the phone and five minutes later another customer walks in and offers you more for it. To protect yourself, you should call the first customer and withdraw your offer before accepting the offer of the second customer. If the first customer accepts before you have withdrawn your offer, you may be sued if you have sold the item to the second customer.

There are a few exceptions to the basic rules of contracts. These are:

- Consent to a contract must be voluntary. If it is made under a threat, the contract is not valid. If a business refuses to give a person's car back unless they pay $200 for changing the oil, the customer could probably sue and get the $200 back.

- Contracts to do illegal acts or acts "against public policy" are not enforceable. If an electrician signs a contract to put some wiring in a house that is not legal, the customer could probably not force him to do it because the court would refuse to require an illegal act.

- If either party to an offer dies, the offer expires and cannot be accepted by the heirs. If a painter is hired to paint a portrait, and dies before completing it, his wife cannot finish it and require payment. However, a corporation does not die, even if its owners die. If a corporation is hired to build a house and the corporation's owner dies, his heirs may take over the corporation and finish the job and require payment.

• Contracts made under misrepresentation are not enforceable. For example, if someone tells you a car has thirty-five thousand miles on it, you agree to buy it, and you later discover it has one hundred thirty-five thousand miles, you may be able to rescind the contract for fraud and misrepresentation.

• If there were a mutual mistake a contract may be rescinded. For example, if both you and the seller thought the car had thirty-five thousand miles on it and both relied on that assumption, the contract could be rescinded. However, if the seller knew the car has one hundred thirty-five thousand miles on it, but you assumed it had thirty-five thousand and did not ask, you probably could not rescind the contract.

STATUTORY CONTRACT LAW

The previous section discussed the basics of contract law. These are not usually stated in the statutes, but are the legal principles decided by judges over hundreds of years. The legislatures in recent times have made numerous exceptions to these principles. In most cases, these laws have been passed when the legislature felt that traditional law was not fair. The important laws which affect contracts are the following:

STATUTES OF FRAUD

Statutes of fraud state when a contract must be in writing to be valid. Some people believe a contract is not valid unless it is in writing, but that is not so. Only those types of contracts mentioned in the statutes of fraud must be in writing. Of course, an oral contract is much harder to prove in court than one that is in writing.

In Massachusetts, some of the contracts that must be in writing, and the applicable statute sections are as follows:

- Sales of any interest in real estate (Mass. Gen. Laws, Ch. 259, Sec. 1)

- Guarantees of debts of another person (Mass. Gen. Laws, Ch. 259, Sec. 1)

- Agreements which take more than one year to complete (Mass. Gen. Laws, Ch. 259, Sec. 1)

- Promises by executors, administrators, or assignees in insolvency to pay damages from their own estates (Mass. Gen. Laws, Ch. 259, Sec. 1)

- Pre-nuptial agreements (Mass. Gen. Laws, Ch. 259, Sec. 1)

- Agreements concerning making or revoking a will or codicil or making a devise (Mass. Gen. Laws, Ch. 259, Sec. 5, 5A)

- Sales of goods over $500 (Mass. Gen. Laws, Ch. 106, Sec. 2-201)

- Sales of personal property of over $5,000 (Mass. Gen. Laws, Ch. 106, Sec. 1-206)

CONSUMER PROTECTION LAW

Because of alleged unfair practices by some types of businesses, laws have been passed controlling the contracts they may use. Most notable among these are agreements for the sale or lease of goods or the rendering of services, or both, primarily for personal, family, or household purposes of over $25 and which are consummated at a place other than the address of the seller or lessor (targeting door-to-door solicitations). These types of agreements may be canceled within three business days. Retail installment sales contracts may also be cancelled within three business days. Motor vehicle retail installment sales contracts may be canceled under certain circumstances. These laws are described in more detail in the section on "Advertising Laws and Rules" in Chapter 11.

PREPARING YOUR CONTRACTS

Before you open your business, you should obtain or prepare the contracts or policies you will use in your business. In some businesses, such as a restaurant, you may not need much. Perhaps you will want a sign near the entrance stating "shirt and shoes required" or "diners must be seated by 10:30 P.M."

However, if you are a building contractor or run a similar business, you will need detailed contracts to use with your customers. If you do not clearly spell out your rights and obligations, you may end up in court and lose thousands of dollars in profits.

Of course, the best way to have an effective contract is to have an attorney, who is experienced in the subject, prepare one to meet the needs of your business. However, since this may be too expensive for your new operation, you may want to go elsewhere. Three sources for the contracts you will need are other business like yours, trade associations, and legal form books. You should obtain as many different contracts as possible, compare them, and decide which terms are most comfortable for you.

INSURANCE

There are not many laws requiring you to have insurance, but if you do not have insurance you may face liability which would ruin your business. You should be aware of the types of insurance available and weigh the risks of a loss against the cost of a policy.

Be aware that there can be a wide range of prices and coverage in insurance policies. You should get at least three quotes from different insurance agents and ask each one to explain the benefits of his or her policy.

WORKERS' COMPENSATION

In general, if you have any employees, you are required by law to carry workers' compensation insurance.

The term "employee" is specifically defined in Massachusetts General Laws, Chapter 152. You should read this law carefully if you think you need to comply with this law. For example, part-time employees, students, aliens, and illegal workers count as employees. However, under certain conditions, professional athletes, real estate agents, part-time domestic workers, seamen, taxi cab drivers, casual and seasonal workers, and door-to-door salespeople are not considered employees. Independent contractors are also not considered employees.

Even if you are not required to have workers' compensation insurance, you may still wish to carry it because it can protect you from litigation.

This insurance can be obtained from most insurance companies and, in many cases, is not expensive. If you have such coverage, you are protected against suits by employees or their heirs in case of an accident, and against potentially ruinous claims.

Failure to provide workers' compensation insurance when required is considered serious. It could result in a substantial fine, prison time, and an injunction against employing anyone. If a person is injured on a job, even if another employee caused it or the injured person contributed to his own injury, you may be required to pay for all resulting losses.

There are other requirements of the workers' compensation law, such as reporting within seven days after notice injuries causing five or more days' loss of work. Also, it is a misdemeanor to deduct the amount of the premiums from the employee's wages.

Unemployment Insurance

Massachusetts requires employers who employ one or more permanent, temporary, or part-time workers to provide information to the Department of Employment and Training regarding its employees. The D.E.T. will determine whether the employer must make unemployment insurance contributions. See the sample in Appendix A on page 202. A blank EMPLOYER STATUS REPORT is contained in Appendix B. (see form 10, p.232.)

The unemployment insurance system is a state system, administered by the Department of Employment and Training. Employers who fail to pay required contributions are subject to various civil and criminal penalties up to $50,000 and five years in jail for certain infractions.

LIABILITY INSURANCE

Liability insurance can be divided into two main areas: coverage for injuries on your premises and by your employees and coverage for injuries caused by your products.

Coverage for the first type of injury is usually very reasonably priced. Injuries in your business or by your employees (such as in an auto accident) are covered by standard premises or auto policies. But coverage for injuries by products may be harder to find and more expensive. In the current liability crisis, juries have awarded ridiculously high judgments for accidents involving products which had little if any impact on the accident. The situation has become so bad that some entire industries have gone out of business or moved overseas.

ASSET PROTECTION

Hopefully, laws will soon be passed to protect businesses from these unfair awards. For now, if insurance is unavailable or unaffordable, you can go without and use a corporation and other asset protection devices to protect yourself from liability.

The best way to find out if insurance is available for your type of business is to check with other businesses. If there is a trade group for your industry, their newsletter or magazine may contain ads for insurers.

UMBRELLA POLICY

As a business owner, you will be a more visible target for lawsuits even if there is little merit to them. Lawyers know that a *nuisance suit* is often settled for thousands of dollars. Because of your greater exposure you should consider getting a personal *umbrella policy*. This is a policy that covers you for claims of up to one, or even two or five, million dollars and is very reasonably priced.

HAZARD INSURANCE

One of the worst things that can happen to your business is a fire, flood, or other disaster. With lost customer lists, inventory, and equipment, many businesses have been forced to close after such a disaster.

The premium for such insurance is usually reasonable and could protect you from loss of your business. You can even get business interruption insurance which will cover your losses while your business is getting back on its feet.

HOME BUSINESS INSURANCE

There is a special insurance problem for home businesses. Most homeowner and tenant insurance policies do not cover business activities. In fact, under some policies you may be denied coverage if you used your home for a business.

If you merely use your home to make business phone calls and send letters, you will probably not have a problem and not need extra coverage. But if you own equipment, or have dedicated a portion of your home exclusively to the business, you could have a problem. Check with your insurance agent for the options that are available to you.

If your business is a sole proprietorship, and you have, say, a computer which you use both personally and for your business, it would probably be covered under your homeowners' policy. But if you incorporate your business and bought the computer in the name of the corporation, coverage might be denied. If a computer is your main business asset you could get a special insurance policy in the company name covering just the computer. One company that offers such a policy is Safeware at 800-723-9273 or 800-800-1492.

AUTOMOBILE INSURANCE

If you or any of your employees will be using an automobile for business purposes, be sure that such use is covered. Sometimes a policy may include an exclusion for business use. Check to be sure your liability policy covers you if one of your employees causes an accident while running a business errand.

HEALTH INSURANCE

While new businesses can rarely afford health insurance for their employees, the sooner they can obtain it, the better chance they will have to find and keep good employees. Those starting a business usually need insurance for themselves (unless they have a working spouse who can cover the family), and they can sometimes get a better rate if they get a small business package. Many local chambers of commerce offer group health insurance plans to small businesses.

EMPLOYEE THEFT

If you fear employees may be able to steal from your business, you may want to have them *bonded*. This means that you pay an insurance company a premium to guarantee employees' honesty, and if they cheat you the insurance company pays you damages. This can cover all existing and new employees.

HEALTH AND
SAFETY LAWS

9

FEDERAL LAWS

OSHA   The *Occupational Safety and Health Administration* (OSHA) is a good example of government regulation so severe it can strangle businesses out of existence. The point of the law is to place the duty on the employer to keep the workplace free from recognized hazards that are likely to cause death or serious bodily injury to workers.

For example, OSHA decided to analyze repetitive-strain injuries, or "RSI," such as carpal tunnel syndrome. The Bureau of Labor Statistics estimated that seven percent of workplace illnesses are RSI and the National Safety Council estimated four percent. OSHA, however, determined that sixty percent is a more accurate figure and came out with a six hundred page list of proposed regulations, guidelines, and suggestions. These regulations would have affected over one-half of all businesses in America and cost billions of dollars. Fortunately, these regulations were shot down by Congress in 1995 after an outcry from businesses. Shortly thereafter, OSHA officials ignored Congress' sentiment and promised to launch a new effort.

Fortunately for small businesses, the regulations are not as cumbersome as those for larger enterprises. If you have ten or fewer employees or if you are in certain types of businesses, you do not have to keep a record of employees' illnesses, injuries, and exposure to hazardous substances. If you have eleven or more employees, you do have to keep this record, which is called *Log 200*. All employers are required to display a poster that you can get from OSHA.

Within forty-eight hours of an on-the-job death of an employee or injury of five or more employees on the job, the area director of OSHA must be contacted.

For more information, you should write or call an OSHA office:

> U.S. Department of Labor
> 200 Constitution Avenue, NW, Room N-3101
> Washington, DC 20210
> Tel. 202-219-4667
> Boston: 617-565-9860

or visit their website at **www.osha-slc.gov** and obtain copies of their publications, *OSHA Handbook for Small Business* (OSHA 2209), and *OSHA Publications and Audiovisual Programs Catalog* (OSHA 2019). They also have a poster that is required to be posted in the workplace at **www.osha-slc.gov/OshDoc/Additional.html**.

HAZARD COMMUNICATION STANDARD

The Hazard Communication Standard requires that employees be made aware of the hazards in the workplace. (Code of Federal Regulations (C.F.R.), Title 29, Section (Sec.) 1910.1200.) It is especially applicable to those working with chemicals but this can include even offices which use copy machines. Businesses using hazardous chemicals must have a comprehensive program for informing employees of the hazards and for protecting them from contamination.

For more information, you can contact OSHA at the previously-mentioned addresses, phone numbers, or websites. They can supply a copy of the regulation and a booklet called *OSHA 3084* which explains the law.

EPA   The Worker Protection Standard for Agricultural Pesticides requires safety training, decontamination sites and, of course, posters. The Environmental Protection Agency will provide information on compliance with this law. They can be reached at:

> Environmental Protection Agency
> 1200 Pennsylvania Ave. NW
> Washington, DC 20460
> 800-490-9198
> www.epa.gov

FDA   The Pure Food and Drug Act of 1906 prohibits the misbranding or adulteration of food and drugs. It also created the Food and Drug Administration (FDA) which has promulgated tons of regulations and which must give permission before a new drug can be introduced into the market. If you will be dealing with any food or drugs you should keep abreast of their policies. Their website is **www.fda.gov**, their small business site is **www.fda.gov/ora/fed_state/small_business/sb_guide /default.htm** and their local small business representative is:

> FDA,Northeast Region
> Small Business Representative (HFR-NE17) Herman Janiger
> 850 Third Ave.
> Brooklyn, NY 11232-1593
> 718-340-700 ext. 5528
> fax: 718-340-7037
> E-mail: hjaniger@ora.fda.gov

HAZARDOUS
MATERIALS
TRANSPORTATION

There are regulations that control the shipping and packing of hazardous materials. For more information contact:

> Office of Hazardous Materials Transportation
> 400 Seventh St. SW
> Washington, DC 20590
> 202-366-8553
> http://hazmat.dot.gov

CPSC

The Consumer Product Safety Commission (CPSC) has a set of rules which cover the safety of products. The commission feels that because its rules cover products, rather than people or companies, they apply to everyone producing such products. However, federal laws do not apply to small businesses which do not affect interstate commerce. Whether a small business would fall under a CPSC rule would depend on the size and nature of your business.

The CPSC rules are contained in The Code of Federal Regulations, Title 16 in the following parts. These can be found at most law libraries, some public libraries, and on the Internet at **www.access.gpo.gov /nara/cfr/cfr-table-search.html**. The CPSC's site is at: **http://cpsc.gov /index.html**.

PRODUCT	PART
Antennas, CB and TV	1402
Architectural Glazing Material	1201
Articles Hazardous to Children Under 3	1501
Baby Cribs-Full Size	1508
Baby Cribs-Non-Full Size	1509
Bicycle Helmets	1203
Bicycles	1512
Carpets and Rugs	1630, 1631
Cellulose Insulation	1209, 1404
Cigarette Lighters	1210
Citizens Band Base Station Antennas	1204

Coal and Wood Burning Appliances	1406
Consumer Products Containing Chlorofluorocarbons	1401
Electrically Operated Toys	1505
Emberizing Materials Containing Asbestos (banned)	1305
Extremely Flammable Contact Adhesives (banned)	1302
Fireworks	1507
Garage Door Openers	1211
Hazardous Lawn Darts (banned)	1306
Hazardous Substances	1500
Human Subjects	1028
Lawn Mowers, Walk-Behind	1205
Lead-Containing Paint (banned)	1303
Matchbooks	1202
Mattresses	1632
Pacifiers	1511
Patching Compounds Containing Asbestos (banned)	1304
Poisons	1700
Rattles	1510
Self-Pressurized Consumer Products	1401
Sleepwear-Children's	1615, 1616
Swimming Pool Slides	1207
Toys, Electrical	1505
Unstable Refuse Bins (banned)	1301

ADDITIONAL REGULATIONS

There are proposals for new laws and regulations every day. It would be impossible to include every conceivable one in this book. To be up to date on the laws that affect your type of business, you should belong to a trade association for your industry and subscribe to newsletters which cover your industry. Attending industry conventions is a good way to learn more and to discover new ways to increase your profits.

MASSACHUSETTS LAWS

SMOKING

Massachusetts has laws which prohibit smoking in the following places:

- public elevators;

- supermarkets and retail food outlets;

- in or upon any public mass transit conveyances or indoor platform or enclosed outdoor platform;

- at any open meeting of a government body;

- any courtroom;

- the State House;

- any building owned by the Commonwealth; and,

- any space occupied by a state agency or department of the Commonwealth.

DESIGNATED
SMOKING AREAS

No one may smoke in any of the following places except in specifically designated smoking areas:

- courthouse
- school
- college
- university
- museum
- library
- train

- waiting area of an airport
- waiting area of a health care facility
- group child care center
- school-aged day care center
- family day care center
- at any public building
- airplane

- any restaurant with a seating capacity of seventy-five or more persons

Areas within the above-listed locations can be designated as a smoking area only if nonsmoking areas of sufficient size and capacity are available to accommodate nonsmokers. Any person admitted to a health care facility must, upon request, be assigned a room in which smoking is not permitted. Notices must be placed at entrances to describe the above smoking prohibitions and to designate smoking areas and no smoking areas.

The law allows smoking in a completely enclosed private office used by an individual within any of the above-listed facilities, public buildings, vehicles, or places except the State House, any building owned by the Commonwealth, and any space occupied by a state agency or department of the Commonwealth (not including state hospitals and substance abuse treatment centers).

Employment and Labor Laws 10

Hiring and Firing Laws

For small businesses, there are not many rules regarding whom you may hire or fire. Fortunately, the ancient law that an employee can be fired at any time (or may quit at any time) still prevails for small businesses. But in certain situations, and as you grow, you will come under a number of laws which affect your hiring and firing practices.

One of the most important things to consider when hiring someone is that if you fire them they may be entitled to unemployment compensation. If so, your unemployment insurance contributions will likely go up and it can cost you a lot of money. Therefore, you should only hire people whom you are sure you will keep, and you should avoid situations where your former employees can collect unemployment.

One way this can be done is by hiring only part-time employees. The drawback to this is that you may not be able to attract the best employees. When hiring dishwashers or busboys this may not be an issue, but when hiring someone to develop a software product, you do not want them to leave halfway through the development.

A better solution is to screen applicants to begin with and only hire those whom you feel certain will succeed. Of course, this is easier said than done. Some people interview well but then turn out to be incompetent at the job.

The best record to look for is someone who has stayed a long time at each of their previous jobs. Next best is someone who has not stayed as long (for good reasons) but has always been employed. The worst type of hire would be someone who is or has been collecting unemployment compensation.

In the authors' experience, the intelligence of an employee is more important than his or her experience. An employee with years of typing experience may be fast but unable to figure out how to use your new computer. On the other hand, an intelligent employee can learn the equipment quickly and eventually gain speed. Of course, common sense is important in all situations.

The bottom line is that you cannot know if an employee will be able to fill your needs from a resumé and interview. Once you have found someone whom you think will work out, offer them a job with a ninety day probationary period. If you are not completely satisfied with them after the ninety days, offer to extend the probationary period for ninety additional days rather than end the relationship immediately. Of course, all of this should be in writing.

BACKGROUND CHECKS

Checking references is important, but beware that a former boss may be a good friend, or even a relative. Some may consider it acceptable to exaggerate on resumés, but in recent years, some applicants have been found to be completely fabricating sections of their education and experience.

POLYGRAPH TESTS

Under the federal *Employee Polygraph Protection Act*, you cannot require an employee or prospective employee to take a polygraph test unless you are in the armored car, guard, or pharmaceutical business. Under Massachusetts law, employers may not use lie detector tests on *any* employee or applicant for employment. Applications must contain a written notice stating that lie detector testing is illegal.

MEDICAL EXAMINATIONS

Employers may conduct medical exams, at the employer's expense, only for the purpose of determining whether the employee is capable of performing the job with reasonable accommodation. Employers may not require AIDS/HIV testing as a condition of employment. Upon request, a copy of the medical report must be furnished to the employee.

DRUG TESTS   Under the ADA, drug testing can only be required of applicants who have been offered jobs conditioned upon passing the drug test. Massachusetts does not have a statute limiting or prohibiting drug testing, but drug tests would be susceptible to challenges under broad statutes such as privacy laws.

FIRING

In most cases, unless you have a contract with an employee for a set time period, you can fire him or her at any time for any or no reason. This is only fair since the employee can quit at any time. The exceptions to this are: if you fired someone based on illegal discrimination (see pages 85–88), for filing some sort of health or safety complaint, or for refusing your sexual advances (see pages 88–91).

NEW HIRE REPORTING

A federal law was passed in 1996 that requires the reporting of new hires. This is the *Personal Responsibility and Work Opportunity Reconciliation Act of 1996* (PRWORA), which provides that such information must be reported by employers to their state government. Massachusetts has had a similar law since 1993.

Massachusetts law requires that within fourteen days of hiring a new employee, an employer must provide the state with information about the employee including the name, social security number, and address. This information can be submitted in several ways including mail, fax, magnetic tape, or over the Internet. There is a special form which can be used for this reporting; however, an employer can use the IRS **W-4 FORM** for this purpose. Since this form must be filled out for all employees anyway, it would be pointless to use a separate form for the new hire reporting. A copy of the **W-4 FORM** is included in the appendix and this may be faxed to 617-887-5049 or mailed to:

> Department of Revenue
> P. O. Box 7032
> Boston, MA 02204

You can call them at 800-332-2733 or visit their website at **www.ma-cse.org** for more information about the program.

EMPLOYMENT AGREEMENTS

To avoid misunderstanding with employees, you should use an employment agreement or an employee handbook. These can spell out in detail the policies of your company and the rights of your employees. They can protect your trade secrets and spell out clearly that employment can be terminated at any time by either party.

While it may be difficult or awkward to ask an existing employee to sign such an agreement, an applicant hoping you will hire them will usually sign whatever is necessary to obtain the job. However, because of the unequal bargaining position, you should not use an agreement which would make you look bad if the matter ever went to court.

If having an employee sign an agreement is awkward, you can usually obtain the same rights by putting the company policies in an employee manual. Each existing and new employee should be given a copy of the manual, along with a letter stating that the rules apply to all employees and that by accepting or continuing employment at your company they agree to abide by the rules. Having an employee sign a receipt for the letter and manual is proof that they received it.

One danger of an employment agreement or handbook is that it may be interpreted to create a long term employment contract. To avoid this, be sure that you clearly state in the agreement or handbook that the employment is "at will" and can be terminated at any time by either party for any or no reason.

Some other things to consider in an employment agreement or handbook are:

- what the salary and other compensation will be;

- what the hours of employment will be;

- what the probationary period will be;

- sexual harassment policy (see pages 90–91);

- that the employee cannot sign any contracts binding the employer; and,

- that the employee agrees to arbitration rather than filing a lawsuit in the event of a dispute.

Independent Contractors

One way to avoid problems with employees and taxes at the same time is to have all of your work done through independent contractors. This can relieve you of most of the burdens of employment laws and the obligation to pay social security and medicare taxes for the workers.

An independent contractor is, in effect, a separate business which you pay to do a job. You pay them just as you pay any company from which you buy products or services. If the amount paid at the end of the year exceeds $600, you will issue an IRS Form 1099 form instead of an IRS Form W-2.

This may seem too good to be true; and in some situations, it is. The IRS does not like *independent contractor* (IC) arrangements because it is too easy for the ICs to cheat on their taxes. To limit the use of ICs, the IRS has strict regulations on who may and may not be classified an independent contractor. Also, companies who do not appear to pay enough in wages for their field of business are often audited.

The highest at-risk jobs are those which are not traditionally done by independent contractors. For example, you could not get away with hiring a secretary as an independent contractor. One of the most important factors considered in determining if a worker can be an independent contractor is the amount of control the company has over his or her work. If you need someone to paint your building and you agree to pay them a certain price to do it according to their own methods and schedule, you can pay them as an independent contractor. But if you tell them when to work, how to do the job, and provide them with the tools and materials, they will be classified an employee.

If you just need some typing done and you take it to a typing service and pick it up when it is ready, you will be safe in treating them as independent contractors. But, if you need someone to come into your office to type on your machine at your schedule, you will probably be required to treat that person as an employee for tax purposes.

The IRS has a form you can use in determining if a person is an employee or an independent contractor, called DETERMINATION OF EMPLOYEE WORK STATUS. It is **IRS FORM SS-8**. (see form 6, p.221.)

INDEPENDENT CONTRACTORS VERSUS EMPLOYEES

In deciding whether to make use of independent contractors or employees, you should weigh the following advantages and disadvantages.

Advantages of using ICs.

- *Lower taxes.* You do not have to pay social security, medicare, unemployment, or other employee taxes.

- *Less paperwork.* You do not have to separate and then send federal withholding deposits or monthly employer returns to the state or federal government.

- *Less insurance.* You do not have to pay workers' compensation insurance and since the workers are not your employees, you do not have to insure against their possible liabilities.

- *More flexibility.* You can use ICs when you need them and not pay them when business is slow.

Disadvantages of using ICs.

- The IRS and state tax offices are strict about when workers may be qualified as ICs. They will audit companies whose use of ICs does not appear to be legitimate.

- If your use of ICs is found to be improper, you may have to pay back taxes and penalties and have problems with your pension plan.

- While employees usually cannot sue you for their injuries (if you have covered them with workers' compensation), ICs can sue you if their injuries were your fault.

- If you are paying someone to produce a creative work (writing, photography, artwork), you receive less rights to the work of an IC.

- You have less control over the work of an IC and less flexibility in terminating them if you are not satisfied that the job is being done the way you require.

- You have less loyalty from an IC who works sporadically for you and possibly others than from your own full time employees.

For some businesses, the advantages outweigh the disadvantages; but for others, they do not. Consider your business plans and the consequences from each type of arrangement. Keep in mind that it will be easier to start with ICs and switch to employees than to hire employees and have to fire them to hire ICs.

TEMPORARY WORKERS

Another way to avoid the hassles of hiring employees is to get workers from a temporary agency. In this arrangement, you may pay a higher amount per hour for the work, but the agency will take care of all of the tax and insurance requirements. Since these can be expensive and time-consuming, the extra per hour cost may be well worth it.

Whether temporary workers will work for you depends upon the type of business you are in and the tasks you need performed. For such jobs as sales management, you would probably want someone who will stay with you long term and develop relationships with the buyers, but for order fulfillment, temporary workers might work out well.

Another advantage of temporary workers is that you can easily stop using those who do not work out well for you, but if you find one who is ideal, you may be able to hire him or her on a full time basis.

In recent years, a new wrinkle has developed in the temporary worker area. Many large companies are beginning to use them because they are so much cheaper than paying the benefits demanded by full time employees. For example, Microsoft Corp. has had as many as 6,000 temporary workers, some of whom worked for them for years. However, some of the temporary workers recently won a lawsuit declaring that they are really employees and are entitled to the same benefits of other employees (such as pension plans).

The law is not yet settled in this area as to what arrangements will result in a temporary worker being declared an employee. That will take several more court cases, some of which have already been filed. A few things you can do to protect yourself are:

- Be sure that all of your benefit plans make it clear that they do not apply to workers obtained through temporary agencies.

- Do not keep the same temporary workers for longer than a year.

- Do not list temporary workers in any employee directories or hold them out to the public as your employees.

- Do not allow them to use your business cards or stationery.

DISCRIMINATION LAWS

FEDERAL LAW   There are numerous federal laws forbidding discrimination based upon race, sex, pregnancy, color, religion, national origin, age, or disability. The laws apply to both hiring and firing, and to employment practices such as salaries, promotions, and benefits. Most of these laws only apply to an employer who has fifteen or more employees for twenty weeks of a calendar year or has federal contracts or subcontracts. Therefore, you most likely will not be required to comply with the law immediately upon opening your business. However, there are similar state laws which may apply to your business.

One exception is the *Equal Pay Act* which applies to employers with two or more employees and requires that women be paid the same as men in the same type of job.

Employers with fifteen or more employees are required to display a poster regarding discrimination. This poster is available from the Equal Employment Opportunity Commission, 2401 E. Street, N.W., Washington, DC 20506. Employers with 100 or more employees are required to file an annual report with the EEOC.

When hiring employees, some questions are illegal or inadvisable to ask. The following questions should not be included on your employment application, or in your interviews, unless the information is somehow directly tied to the duties of the job:

- Do not ask about an applicant's citizenship or place of birth. But after hiring an employee you must ask about his or her right to work in this country.

- Do not ask a female applicant her maiden name. You can ask if she has been known by any other name in order to do a background check.

- Do not ask if applicants have children, plan to have them, or have child care. You can ask if an applicant will be able to work the required hours.

- Do not ask if the applicant has religious objections to working Saturday or Sunday. You can mention if the job requires such hours and ask whether the applicant can meet this job requirement.

- Do not ask an applicant's age. You can ask if an applicant is eighteen or over, or for a liquor-related job if they are twenty-one or over.

- Do not ask an applicant's weight.

- Do not ask if an applicant has AIDS or is HIV positive.

- Do not ask if the applicant has filed a workers' compensation claim.

- Do not ask about the applicant's previous health problems.

- Do not ask if the applicant is married or whether their spouse would object to the job, hours, or duties.

- Do not ask if the applicant owns a home, furniture, car, as it is considered racially-discriminatory.

- Do not ask if the applicant was ever arrested. You can ask if the applicant was ever convicted of a crime.

The most recent, and perhaps most onerous, law is the *Americans with Disabilities Act* (ADA) of 1990. Under this law, employers who do not make "reasonable accommodations for disabled employees" will face fines of up to $100,000, as well as other civil penalties and civil damage awards.

While the goal of creating more opportunities for people with disabilities is a good one, the result of this law is to place all of the costs of achieving this goal on businesses that are faced with disabled applicants. For example, it has been suggested that the requirement of "reasonable accommodation" will require some companies to hire blind applicants for jobs which require reading and then to hire second employees to read to the blind employees. We will only know the extent to which this law can be applied after some employers have been taken to court.

A study released by two MIT economists in late 1998 indicated that since the ADA was passed, employers have hired fewer rather than more disabled people. It is theorized that this may be due the the expense of the "reasonable accommodations" or the fear of lawsuits by disabled employees.

The ADA currently applies to employers with fifteen or more employees. Employers who need more than fifteen employees might want to consider contracting with independent contractors to avoid problems with this law, particularly if the number of employees is only slightly larger than fifteen.

To find out how this law affects your business, you might want to pay the government $25 for its *ADA Technical Assistance Manual*. You can order it from The Superintendent of Documents, P. O. Box 371954, Pittsburgh, PA 15250-7954, or you can fax your credit card order to 202-512-2233.

Tax benefits. There are three types of tax credits to help small business with the burden of these laws.

- Businesses can deduct up to $15,000 a year for making their premises accessible to the disabled and can depreciate the rest (IRC sec. 190).

- Small businesses (under $1,000,000 in revenue and under thirty employees) can get a tax credit each year for fifty percent of the cost of making their premises accessible to the disabled, but this only applies to the amount between $250 and $10,500.

- Small businesses can get a credit of up to forty percent of the first $6,000 of wages paid to certain new employees who qualify. See **IRS form 8850** and instructions.

Records. To protect against potential claims of discrimination, all employers should keep detailed records showing reasons for hiring or not hiring applicants and for firing employees.

MASSACHUSETTS
LAW

Massachusetts has its own laws regarding discrimination in employment practices. Chapter 151B of the Massachusetts General Laws, which applies to employers with six or more employees, prohibits discrimination or classification based upon race, color, religion, sex, national origin, age, sexual orientation (excluding persons whose sexual orientation involves minor children as the sex object), ancestry, handicap, or marital status, unless based on a bona fide occupational qualification. It is also unlawful to require someone, as a condition of obtaining or keeping employment, to violate or forgo the practice of his creed or religion, including the observance of any particular holy day. "Reasonable accommodation" by the employer is required. An employer who violates these laws can be sued and be required to pay back pay, damages, and punitive damages.

SEXUAL HARASSMENT

FEDERAL LAW

What began as protection for employees who were fired or not promoted for failing to succumb to sexual advances of their superiors has been expanded to outlaw nearly any sexual comments or references in the workplace. (One university was even forced to take down a painting by Goya depicting a nude because a teacher felt sexually harassed by its presence.)

In the 1980s, the Equal Employment Opportunity Commission interpreted the Title VII of the Civil Rights Act of 1964 to forbid sexual harassment. After that, the courts took over and reviewed all types of conduct in the workplace. The numerous lawsuits that followed began a trend toward expanding the definition of sexual harassment and favoring employees.

The EEOC has held the following in sexual harassment cases:

- The victim as well as the harasser may be a woman or a man.

- The victim does not have to be of the opposite sex.

- The harasser can be the victim's supervisor, an agent of the employer, a supervisor in another area, a co-worker, or a non-employee.

- The victim does not have to be the person harassed, but could be anyone affected by the offensive conduct.

- Unlawful sexual harassment may occur without economic injury to or discharge of the victim.

- The harasser's conduct must be unwelcome.

Some of the actions that have been considered harassment are:

- displaying sexually explicit posters in the workplace;

- requiring female employees to wear revealing uniforms;

- rating of sexual attractiveness of female employees as they passed male employees' desks; and,

- continued sexual jokes and innuendos;

- demands for sexual favors from subordinates;

- unwelcomed sexual propositions or flirtation;

- unwelcomed physical contact; and,

- whistling or leering at members of the opposite sex.

In 1993, the United States Supreme Court ruled that an employee can make a claim for sexual harassment even without proof of a specific injury. However, lower federal courts in more recent cases (such as the Paula Jones case against President Clinton) have dismissed cases where no specific injury was shown (although these cases may be overruled by a higher court). These new cases may indicate that the pendulum has stopped moving toward expanded rights for the employee.

On the other hand, another recent case ruled that an employer can be liable for the harassment of an employee by a supervisor, even if the employer was unaware of the supervisor's conduct, if the employer did not have a system in place to allow complaints against harassment. This area of law is still developing and to avoid a possible lawsuit you should be aware of the things which could potentially cause liability and avoid them.

Some things a business can do to protect against claims of sexual harassment are:

- distribute a written policy against all kinds of sexual harassment to all employees (this is required in Massachusetts—see below);

- encourage employees to report all incidents of sexual harassment;

- insure there is no retaliation against those who complain;

- make clear that your policy is "zero tolerance;"

- explain that sexual harassment includes both requests for sexual favors and a work environment that some employees may consider hostile;

- allow employees to report harassment to someone other than their immediate supervisor in case that person is involved in the harassment; and,

- promise as much confidentiality as possible to complainants.

MASSACHUSETTS LAW
Massachusetts requires all employers with six or more employees to adopt a written policy against sexual harassment. The written policy must include:

- a statement that sexual harassment in the workplace is unlawful; '

- a statement that it is unlawful to retaliate against an employee for filing a complaint of sexual harassment or for cooperating in an investigation of a complaint for sexual harassment;

- a description and examples of sexual harassment;

- a statement of the range of consequences for employees who are found to have committed sexual harassment;

- a description of the process for filing internal complaints about sexual harassment and the work addresses and telephone numbers of the person or persons to whom complaints should be made; and,

- the identity of the appropriate state and federal employment discrimination enforcement agencies and directions as to how to contact them.

Employers must provide all new employees with a copy of the policy when they commence employment and must provide each employee a copy annually. The law required the Massachusetts Commission Against Discrimination to prepare a model policy which conforms with the federal and state requirements. It is reproduced at the end of the chapter.

COMMON LAW
Although the federal and civil rights laws only apply to businesses with fifteen or more employees, and the Massachusetts laws to businesses with six or more employees, any employee could sue for sexual harassment in civil court. However, this is difficult and expensive, and would only be worthwhile where there were substantial damages.

WAGE AND HOUR LAWS

FEDERAL LAW
Businesses covered. The *Fair Labor Standards Act* (FLSA) applies to all employers who are engaged in "interstate commerce" or in the production of goods for interstate commerce (anything which will cross the state line) and all employees of hospitals, schools, residential facilities for the disabled or aged, or public agencies. It also applies to all employees of enterprises that gross $500,000 or more per year.

While many small businesses might not think they are engaged in interstate commerce, the laws have been interpreted so broadly that nearly any use of the mails, interstate telephone service, or other interstate services, however minor, is enough to bring a business under the law. The authors of our Constitution clearly intended for most rights to be reserved to the states, but the *commerce clause* has been used to expand federal control to many unintended areas.

Minimum wage. The federal wage and hour laws are contained in the Federal Fair Labor Standards Act. At this time (i.e., the time this book was printed), the minimum wage is $5.15 per hour. In certain circumstances, a wage of $3.62 may be paid to employees under twenty years of age for a ninety day training period. For employees who regularly receive more than $30 a month in tips, the minimum wage is $2.13 per hour. But if the employee's tips do not bring him up to the full $5.15 minimum wage, then the employer must make up the difference.

Overtime. Workers who work over forty hours in a week must be paid time-and-a-half for the time worked over forty hours.

Exempt employees. While nearly all businesses are covered, certain employees are exempt from the FLSA. Exempt employees include employees that are considered executives, administrative and managerial, professionals, computer professionals, and outside salespeople.

Whether one of these exceptions applies to a particular employee is a complicated legal question. Thousands of court cases have been decided on this issue but they have given no clear answers. In one case a person could be determined to be exempt because of his duties, but in another, a person with the same duties could be found not exempt.

One thing that is clear is that the determination is made on the employee's function, and not just the job title. You cannot make a secretary exempt by calling her a manager if most of her duties are clerical. For more information contact:

Wage and Hour Division
U. S. Department of Labor
200 Constitution Ave., N.W. Room S-3325
Washington, DC 20210
617-565-2072.
www.dol.gov/dol/esa/public/whd_org.htm

On the Internet, you can obtain information on the Department of Labor's Small Business Handbook at: **www.dol.gov/dol/asp/public /programs/handbook/main.htm**.

MASSACHUSETTS LAW

Massachusetts requires a minimum wage of $6.75 per hour, except in particular specified occupations. The Commissioner of Labor may set lower minimum rates for certain occupations, but may not set a rate lower than a specified amount per hour except for learners, apprentices, ushers, ticket sellers and takers, janitors, caretakers, golf caddies, and service people earning more than $20 a month in tips.

Most employees are entitled to time-and-a-half for hours worked over forty per week. Most employers must pay wages at least every two weeks, or pay no later than six days after the last day worked.

State, county, and certain municipal employees may not work more than eight hours a day, forty-eight hours a week, and six days a week, except in case of emergency.

Private employers must give employees in certain occupations twenty-four consecutive hours to rest every seven consecutive days. There are also restrictions on requiring employees to work on Sundays or holidays. Generally, employers must allow a thirty minute meal break for each six hours of work.

PENSION AND BENEFIT LAWS

There are no laws requiring small businesses to provide any types of special benefits to employees. Such benefits are given to attract and keep good employees. With pension plans the main concern is if you do start one it must comply with federal tax laws.

HOLIDAYS

There are no federal or Massachusetts laws which require that employees be given holidays off. You can require them to work Thanksgiving and Christmas and dock their pay or fire them for failing to show. Of course, you will not have much luck keeping employees with such a policy.

Most companies give full time employees a certain number of paid holidays, such as: New Year's Day (January 1); Memorial Day (last Monday in May); Fourth of July; Labor Day (first Monday in September); Thanksgiving (fourth Thursday in November) and Christmas (December 25). Some, but not many, employers include other holidays such as Martin Luther King, Jr.'s birthday (January 15); President's Day; and Columbus Day. If one of the holidays falls on a Saturday or Sunday, many employers give the preceding Friday or following Monday off.

Massachusetts law says that legal holidays include the following:

New Year's Day (January 1)

Independence Day (July 4)

Veteran's Day (November 11)

Christmas Day (December 25)

(or the day following when any of said days occurs on Sunday)

Martin Luther King, Jr.'s Birthday (3rd Monday in January)

George Washington's Birthday (3rd Monday in February)

Patriot's Day (3rd Monday in April)

Memorial Day (last Monday in May)

Labor Day (1st Monday in September)

Columbus Day (2nd Monday in October)

Thanksgiving Day (4th Thursday in November)

With respect to Suffolk County only, Evacuation Day on March 17th (for certain purposes only) and Bunker Hill Day on June 17th, or the day following when said days occur on Sunday, are also legal holidays.

However, the fact that these are designated state holidays does not mean that private employers, other than owners of mills and factories, must observe them. In fact, not even the state government is closed on all of these days.

SICK DAYS

There is no federal or Massachusetts law mandating that an employee be paid for time that he or she is home sick. The situation seems to be that the larger the company, the more paid sick leave is allowed. Part time workers rarely get sick leave and small business sick leave is usually limited for the simple reason that they cannot afford to pay for time that employees do not work.

Some small companies have an official policy of no paid sick leave, but when an important employee misses a day because he or she is clearly sick, it is paid.

PENSION PLANS AND RETIREMENT ACCOUNTS

Few small new businesses can afford to provide pension plans for their employees. The first concern of many small business owners is usually how the owner can shelter income in a pension plan without having to set up a pension plan for an employee. Under most pension plans, this is not allowed.

IRA. Anyone with $2,000 of earnings can put up to that amount in an Individual Retirement Account. Unless the person or his or her spouse is covered by a company pension plan and has income over a certain amount, the amount put into the account is fully tax deductible.

ROTH IRA. Contributions to a Roth IRA are not tax deductible but then when the money is taken out it is not taxable. People who expect to still have taxable income when they withdraw from their IRA can benefit from these.

SEP IRA, SAR-SEP IRA, SIMPLE IRA. With these types of retirement accounts, a person can put a much greater amount into a retirement plan and deduct it from their taxable income. Employees must also be covered by such plans, but certain employees are exempt so it is sometimes possible to use these for the owners alone. The best source for more information is a mutual fund company (such as Vanguard, Fidelity, Dreyfus, etc.) or a local bank, which can set up the plan and provide you with all of the rules. These have an advantage over qualified plans (discussed below) since they do not have the high annual fees. One Internet site which contains some useful information on these accounts is: **www.retirement-information.com/iraaccts.htm.**

Qualified Retirement Plans. Qualified retirement plans are 401(k) plans, Keough plans, and corporate retirement plans. These are covered by ERISA, the Employee Retirement Income Security Act which is a complicated law meant to protect employee pension plans. Congress did not want employees who contributed to pension plans all their lives ending up with nothing when the plan goes bankrupt. The law is so complicated and the penalties so severe that some companies are cancelling their pension plans, and applications for new plans are a fraction of what they were previously. However, many banks and mutual funds have created "canned plans" which can be used instead of drafting one from scratch. Still the fees for administering them are steep. Check with a bank or mutual fund for details.

FAMILY AND MEDICAL LEAVE LAW

FEDERAL LAW

Since Congress thinks business owners are not capable of deciding what type of leave to offer their employees, it passed the Family and Medical Leave Act of 1993. This law requires an employee to be given up to twelve weeks of unpaid leave when:

- the employee or employee's spouse has a child;
- the employee adopts a child or takes in a foster child;
- the employee needs to care for an ill spouse, child, or parent; or,
- the employee becomes seriously ill.

Fortunately, the law only applies to employers with fifty or more employees. Also, the top ten percent of an employer's salaried employees can be denied this leave because of the disruption in business their absence could cause.

MASSACHUSETTS
LAW

Massachusetts law requires employers of six or more employees to give up to eight weeks of maternity leave (but does not require pay during the period) for female employees for the purpose of giving birth or adopting a child under eighteen years of age, or under twenty-three years of age if mentally or physically disabled, provided the employee gives at least two weeks' notice and intends to return to work. Notice of this provision must be posted in the workplace.

Employees of manufacturing, mechanical, or mercantile establishments must be given at leave to vote in any election during the first two hours after the polls are open, upon request. The law also requires leave in certain circumstances for training for armed forces reserves, participation in Veteran's Day or Memorial Day exercises, and jury duty.

In August of 1998, a new statute became effective in Massachusetts, entitled "An Act Providing Employee Leave for Certain Family Obligations." The act, commonly referred to as the *Small Necessities Leave Act* (SNLA), is applicable only to employers who are covered by the federal *Family and Medical Leave Act of 1993* (FMLA).

The SNLA grants an eligible employee up to twenty-four hours of leave during any twelve-month period, in addition to leave under the FMLA, to:

- participate in school activities directly related to the educational advancement of a son or daughter of the employee, such as parent-teacher conferences or interviewing for a new school;

- accompany the son or daughter of the employee to routine medical or dental appointments, such as check-ups or vaccinations; or,

- accompany an elderly relative of the employee to routine medical or dental appointments or appointments for other professional services related to the elder's care, such as interviewing at nursing or group homes.

An *elderly relative* is defined as someone at least sixty years of age who is related by blood or marriage to the employee. A *school* is defined as a public or private elementary or secondary school, a Head Start program, or a state-licensed children's daycare facility.

There are various options to employers for determining the twelve month period, and certain notice requirements.

CHILD LABOR LAWS

FEDERAL LAW
The Federal Fair Labor Standards Act also contains rules regarding the hiring of children. The basic rules are that children under sixteen years old may not be hired at all except in a few jobs such as acting and newspaper delivery, and those under eighteen may not be hired for dangerous jobs. Children may not work more than three hours a day/eighteen hours a week in a school week or more than eight hours a day/forty hours a week in a non-school week. If you plan to hire children, you should check the Federal Fair Labor Standards Act which is in Chapter 29, United States Code (29 USC) and also the related regulations which are in Chapter 29 of the Code of Federal Regulations (29 CFR).

MASSACHUSETTS LAW
Massachusetts also has its own child labor laws, as follows:

Child labor (M.G.L.C. 149, sec. 56-105). The following rules apply to child labor in Massachusetts in addition to federal laws:

- Persons under eighteen generally may not work more than nine hours a day, forty-eight hours a week, or six days a week. In most cases, a child's hours of work each day must fall within ten consecutive hour period. These rules do not apply to professional, executive, administrative or supervisory, and personal secretarial positions.

- 16 and 17 year olds can work only between 6 A.M. and 10 P.M., except in restaurants; they may also work in restuarants until midnight on Fridays, Saturdays and during school vacations, except the last day of vacation; generally, they cannot work more than forty-eight hours a week, nine hours a day, or six days a week.

- 14 and 15 year olds can work only between 7 A.M. and 7 P.M. during the school year, and between 7 A.M. and 9 P.M. during the summer, and not during school hours; generally, they cannot work more than eighteen hours a week, three hours a day on school days, eight hours a day on Saturdays, Sundays and holidays, or six days a week.

- Children are allowed to work up to fifty-two hours per week in certain types of seasonal employment from June to October.

● Children fourteen or younger may work in agricultural labor for up to four hours a day or twenty-four hours a week, or more if related to the owner or operator of farm.

● Children under sixteen may not work on certain equipment and in certain hazardous, arduous or corruptive occupations, or in occupations which may unduly interfere with their schooling.

Hazardous occupations. No persons under eighteen years of age may work in the following occupations or use this equipment:

● blast furnaces;

● hoisting machines;

● oiling or cleaning hazardous machinery in motion;

● polishing or buffing wheels;

● switch tending;

● gate tending;

● track repairing;

● brakeman, fireman, engineer, motorman, or conductor on railroad;

● fireman or engineer on boat;

● operating motor vehicles except in auto repair shop;

● gunpowder and other explosive manufacturing;

● manufacture of phosphorus or phosphorous matches;

● distillery, brewery or other bottling, manufacturing or packing of alcoholic beverages;

● logging or sawmilling;

● selling alcoholic beverages;

● at heights of more than thirty feet above the floor of a room or above ground or water level; or,

● operating, cleaning, or repairing elevators.

IMMIGRATION LAWS

FEDERAL LAW

A law was passed in 1986 by Congress which imposes stiff penalties for any business which hires aliens who are not eligible to work. Under this law, you must verify both the identity and the employment eligibility of anyone you hire by using the EMPLOYMENT ELIGIBILITY VERIFICATION form, IRS FORM I-9. (see form 4, p.218.) Both you and the employee must fill out the form and you must check an employee's identification cards or papers. Fines for hiring illegal aliens range from $250 to $2,000 for the first offense and up to $10,000 for the third offense. Failure to maintain the proper paperwork may result in a fine of up to $1,000. The law does not apply to independent contractors with whom you may contract and it does not penalize you if the employee used fake identification.

There are also penalties which apply to employers of four or more persons for discriminating against eligible applicants because they appear foreign or because of their national origin or citizenship status.

Appendix A includes a sample filled-in IRS FORM I-9, instructions, and a list of acceptable documentation. A blank form is in Appendix B. (see form 4, p.218.) The blank form can also be downloaded from the following website: **www.irs.gov**.

For more information, call 202-514-2000 for the *Handbook for Employers and Instructions for Completing Form I-9*, check the INS web site (**www.ins.usdoj.gov**) or write to the following address:

> U. S. Department of Justice
> Immigration and Naturalization Service
> 425 I Street, NW
> Washington, DC 20536

The Illegal Immigration Reform and Immigrant Responsibility Act of 1996 (IIRIRA) required changes in the rules, but as of early 1999 the INS had not yet promulgated final versions of the rules. The interim rule made the following changes to the requirements:

- remove documents 2, 3, 8, and 9 from column A;

- allow document 4 only for aliens authorized to work for a specific employer; and,

- new rules for employees who do not have their original documents.

However, no new forms or instructions have been made available and employers are not yet being prosecuted for violations of these changes. Employers can receive updates to these laws by fax. To receive them, send your name address and fax number to 202-305-2523.

Foreign employees. If you wish to hire employees who are foreign citizens and are not able to provide the documentation explained above, they must first obtain a work visa from the Immigration and Naturalization Service (INS) of the United States Department of Justice.

Work visas for foreigners are not easy to get. Millions of people around the globe would like to come to the U.S. to work and the laws are designed to keep most of them out to protect the jobs of American citizens.

Whether or not a person can get a work visa depends on whether there is a shortage of U.S. workers available to fill the job. For jobs requiring few or no skills, it is practically impossible to get a visa. For highly skilled jobs, such as nurses, physical therapists, and for those of exceptional ability, such as Nobel Prize winners and Olympic medalists, obtaining a visa is fairly easy.

There are several types of visas and different rules for different countries. For example, NAFTA has made it easier for some types of workers to enter the U.S. from Canada and Mexico. For some positions the shortage of workers is assumed by the INS. For others, a business must first advertise a position available in the U.S. Only after no qualified persons apply, can it hire someone from another country.

The visa system is complicated and subject to regular change. (In late 2000 a new law expanded the number of certain worker visas from 115,000 to 195,000.) If you wish to hire a foreign worker you should consult with an immigration specialist or a book on the subject.

MASSACHUSETTS LAW   Massachusetts General Laws, Chapter 149, Section 19C makes it illegal to hire aliens who are not legally authorized to work.

HIRING "OFF THE BOOKS"

Because of the taxes, insurance, and red tape involved with hiring employees, some new businesses hire people "off the books." They pay them in cash and never admit they are employees. While the cash paid in wages would not be deductible, they consider this a smaller cost than compliance. Some even use "off the books" receipts to cover it.

Except when your spouse or child is giving you some temporary help, this is a terrible idea. Hiring people off the books can result in civil fines, loss of insurance coverage, and even criminal penalties. When engaged in dangerous work like roofing or using power tools, you are risking millions of dollars in potential liability if a worker is killed or seriously injured.

It may be more costly and time consuming to comply with the employment laws, but if you are concerned about long term growth with less risk, it is the wiser way to go.

FEDERAL CONTRACTS

Companies that do work for the federal government are subject to several laws.

DAVIS-BACON ACT   The *Davis-Bacon Act* requires contractors engaged in U.S. government construction projects to pay wages and benefits which are equal to or better than the prevailing wages in the area.

McNAMARA-
O'HARA SERVICE
CONTRACT ACT

The *McNamara-O'Hara Service Contract Act* sets wages and other labor standards for contractors furnishing services to agencies of the U.S. government.

WALSH-HEALEY
PUBLIC
CONTRACTS ACT

The *Walsh-Healey Public Contracts Act* requires the Department of Labor to settle disputes regarding manufacturers supplying products to the U.S. government.

MISCELLANEOUS LAWS

FEDERAL LAW

Affirmative action. In most cases, the federal government does not yet tell employers who they must hire. This would be especially true for small new businesses. The only situation where a small business would need to comply with affirmative action requirements would be if it accepted federal contracts or subcontracts. These requirements could include the hiring of minorities or Vietnam veterans.

Layoffs. Companies with one hundred or more full-time employees at one location are subject to the *Worker Adjustment and Retraining Notification Act*. This law requires a sixty-day notification prior to certain lay-offs and has other strict provisions.

Unions. The *National Labor Relations Act of 1935* gives employees the right to organize a union or to join one. (U.S.C., Title 29, beginning with Sec. 151.) There are things employers can do to protect themselves, but you should consult a labor attorney or a book on the subject before taking action which might be illegal and result in fines.

Poster laws. Yes, there are laws regarding what posters you may or may not display in the workplace. A federal judge ruled in 1991 that Playboy posters in a workplace were sexual harassment. This ruling is being appealed by the American Civil Liberties Union (ACLU). However, there are other poster laws which require certain posters to be displayed to inform employees of their rights. Not all businesses are required to display all posters, but the following list should be of help.

- All employers must display the wage and hour poster available from:

  U. S. Department of Labor
  200 Constitution Ave., NW
  Washington, DC 20210

- Employers with fifteen or more employees for twenty weeks of the year must display the sex, race, religion, and ethnic discrimination poster and the age discrimination poster available from:

  EEOC
  2401 E Street NW
  Washington, DC 20506

- Employers with federal contracts or subcontracts of $10,000 or more must display the sex, race, etc. discrimination poster mentioned above plus a poster regarding Vietnam era veterans available from the local federal contracting office.

- Employers with government contracts subject to the *Service Contract Act* or the *Public Contracts Act* must display a notice to employees working on government contracts available from:

  Employment Standards Division
  U. S. Department of Labor
  200 Constitution Ave., NW
  Washington, DC 20210

MASSACHUSETTS
LAW

Working conditions. Employers must provide proper ventilation, sanitation and lighting, and heat from October 15 to May 15. Industrial and construction workers must be provided drinking water. Fire exits must be accessible during working hours.

Personnel records. Employers must, upon written request of present and former employees, allow those persons to inspect and copy their personnel records.

Prevention of employment. No one may, by intimidation or force, prevent or seek to prevent a person from entering into or continuing in the employment of any person.

Coercion of agreement not to join a labor organization. No one may, himself or by his agent, coerce or compel a person into an agreement not to join or become a member of a labor organization as a condition of his securing employment or continuing employment.

Volunteer experience. Employment applications requiring the applicant to set forth his experience history must contain a statement that the applicant may include in such history any verified work performed on a volunteer basis.

Seats. Employers must provide seats for employees and must allow their use when not engaged in active duties of employment, and while at work unless sitting would interfere with the work or cause danger.

ADVERTISING AND PROMOTION LAWS

11

ADVERTISING LAWS AND RULES

FEDERAL LAWS

The federal government regulates advertising through the Federal Trade Commission (FTC). The rules are contained in the Code of Federal Regulations (C.F.R.). You can find these rules in most law libraries and many public libraries. If you plan any advertising which you think may be questionable, you might want to check the rules. If you question it, most likely the Washington bureaucrats have forbidden it. As you read the rules below, you will probably think of many violations you see every day.

Federal rules do not apply to every business. Small businesses that operate only within one state and do not use the postal service may be exempt. However, many of the federal rules are encompassed by Massachusetts' unfair trade practices laws. Therefore, a violation could be prosecuted by the state rather than the federal government.

Some of the important rules are summarized below. If you wish to learn more details about the rules you should obtain copies from your library.

Deceptive pricing. When prices are being compared, it is required that actual and not inflated prices are used. For example, if an object would usually be sold for $7, you should not first offer it for $10 and then start offering it at thirty percent off. It is considered misleading to suggest that a discount from list price is a bargain if the item is seldom actually sold at list price. If most surrounding stores sell an item for $7, it is considered misleading to say it has a "retail value of $10" even if there are some stores elsewhere selling it at that price. (Code of Federal Regulations (C.F.R.), Title 16, Chapter (Ch.) I, Part 233.)

Bait advertising. Bait advertising is placing an ad when you don't really want the respondents to buy the product offered, but to switch to another item. The factors used to determine if there was a violation are similar to those used by Massachusetts in applying its unfair trade practices laws. (C.F.R., Title 16, Ch. I, Part 238.)

Use of "free," "half-off," and similar words. Use of words such as "free," "1¢ sale" and the like must not be misleading. This means that the "regular price" must not include a mark-up to cover the "free" item. The seller must expect to sell the product without the free item at some time in the future. (How many violations of this rule can you find in today's paper?) (C.F.R., Title 16, Ch. I, Part 251.)

Substantiation of claims. The FTC requires that advertisers be able to substantiate their claims. Some information on this policy is contained on the Internet at **www.ftc.gov/bcp/guides/ad3subst.htm**. (CFR, Title 16, Section (Sec.) 3.40 and C.F.R., Title 48, Sec. 10471, 1983.)

Endorsements. This rule forbids endorsements which are misleading. An example is a quote from a film review which is used in such a way as to change the substance of the review. It is not necessary to use the exact words of the person endorsing the product as long as the opinion is not distorted. If a product is changed, an endorsement which does not apply to the new version cannot be used. For some items, such as drugs, claims cannot be used without scientific proof. Endorsements by organizations cannot be used unless one is sure that the membership holds the same opinion. (C.F.R., Title 16, Ch. I, Part 255.)

Unfairness. Any advertising practices which can be deemed to be "unfair" are forbidden by the FTC. An explanation of this policy is located on the Internet at **www.ftc.gov/bcp/policystmt/ad-unfair.htm**. (U.S.C., Title 15, Sec. 45.)

Negative option plans. When a seller uses a sales system in which the buyer must notify the seller if he does not want the goods, the seller must provide the buyer with a form to decline the sale and at least ten days in which to decline. Bonus merchandise must be shipped promptly and the seller must promptly terminate any who so request after completion of the contract. (C.F.R. 16 Ch. I Part 425.)

Laser eye surgery. Under the laws governing deceptive advertising, the FTC and the FDA are regulating the advertising of laser eye surgery. Anyone involved in this area should obtain a copy of these rules. The are located on the Internet at **www.ftc.gov/bcp/guides/eyecare2.htm**. (U.S.C., Title 15, Sec. 45, 52–57.)

Food and dietary supplements. Under the Nutritional Labeling Education Act of 1990, the FTC and the FDA regulate the packaging and advertising of food and dietary products. Anyone involved in this area should obtain a copy of these rules. The are located on the Internet at **www.ftc.gov/bcp/guides/ad4diet.htm** and **www.ftc.gov/bcp/guides /ad-food.htm**. (U.S.C., Title 21, Sec. 343.)

Jewelry and precious metals. The FTC has numerous rules governing the sale and advertising of jewelry and precious metals. Anyone in this business should obtain a copy of these rules. The are located on the Internet at: **www.ftc.gov/bcp/guides/jewel-gd.htm**. (C.F.R., Title 61, Sec. 27212.)

MASSACHUSETTS LAWS

Massachusetts has unfair trade practices laws which provide for treble damages for consumers against businesses which have willfully or knowingly violated the law. Among the prohibited actions are the following:

- Advertising goods at less than cost plus sales tax for the purpose of injuring or destroying competition (with exceptions).

- Failure by a merchant to disclose any fact, the disclosure of which may have influenced the buyer not to enter into the transaction to start with.

- Failure by a merchant in advertising to disclose all material facts concerning the product or service which, if not disclosed, might directly or by implication, mislead the consumer.

- Making any claim or representation by any means which has the capacity or tendency or effect of deceiving buyers or prospective buyers as to the value or the past, present, common or usual price of a product, or as to any reduction in price of a product, or any saving relating to a product.

- A statement or illustration in an advertisement which creates a false impression of the grade, quality, make, value, currency of model, size, color, usability, or origin of the product offered, or which may otherwise misrepresent the product in such a manner that later, on disclosure of the true facts, there is a likelihood that the buyer may be switched from the advertised product to another.

- Engaging in any act or practice to discourage the purchase of the advertised product as part of a bait scheme to sell another product.

- Car dealers' forcing customers to purchase optional accessories installed by the dealer.

- Negligent misrepresentation of fact when the truth is reasonably capable of ascertainment. This might include the following things:

  - misrepresenting the owner, manufacturer, distributor, source, or geographical origin of goods;

  - misrepresenting the age, model, grade, style, or standard of goods;

  - misrepresenting the sponsorship, endorsement, approval, or certification of goods or services;

  - misrepresenting the affiliation, connection, or association of any goods or services;

  - misrepresenting the nature, characteristics, standard ingredients, uses, benefits, warranties, guarantees, quantities, or qualities of goods or services;

- misrepresenting used, altered, deteriorated, or repossessed goods as new;

- disparaging goods, services, or business of another by false or misleading representation; or,

- advertising goods or services with intent not to sell them as advertised.

INTERNET SALES LAWS

There are not yet specific laws governing Internet transactions which are different from laws governing other transactions. The FTC feels that its current rules regarding deceptive advertising, substantiation, disclaimers, refunds, and related matters must be followed by Internet businesses and that consumers are adequately protected by them. See the first three pages of this chapter for that information.

For some specific guidelines on Internet advertising, see the FTC's site at http://ftc.gov/bcp/conline/pubs/buspubs/ruleroad.htm.

HOME SOLICITATION LAWS

FEDERAL LAW   The Federal Trade Commission has rules governing door-to-door sales. It is a deceptive trade practice in any such sale to fail to furnish a receipt explaining the sale (in the language of the presentation). It is also deceptive not to give notice that there is a right to back out of the contract within three days, known as a *right of rescission*. The notice must be supplied in duplicate, must be in at least ten-point type, and must be captioned either "Notice of Right to Cancel" or "Notice of Cancellation." The notice must be worded as follows on the next page:

NOTICE OF CANCELLATION

_____

Date

YOU MAY CANCEL THIS TRANSACTION, WITHOUT ANY PENALTY OR OBLIGATION, WITHIN THREE BUSINESS DAYS FROM THE ABOVE DATE.

IF YOU CANCEL, ANY PROPERTY TRADED IN, ANY PAYMENTS MADE BY YOU UNDER THE CONTRACT OR SALE, AND ANY NEGOTIABLE INSTRUMENT EXECUTED BY YOU WILL BE RETURNED TO YOU WITHIN 10 BUSINESS DAYS FOLLOWING RECEIPT BY THE SELLER OF YOUR CANCELLATION NOTICE, AND ANY SECURITY INTEREST ARISING OUT OF THE TRANSACTION WILL BE CANCELLED.

IF YOU CANCEL, YOU MUST MAKE AVAILABLE TO THE SELLER AT YOUR RESIDENCE, IN SUBSTANTIALLY AS GOOD CONDITION AS WHEN RECEIVED, ANY GOODS DELIVERED TO YOU UNDER THIS CONTRACT OR SALE; OR YOU MAY IF YOU WISH, COMPLY WITH THE INSTRUCTIONS OF THE SELLER REGARDING THE RETURN SHIPMENT OF THE GOODS AT THE SELLER'S EXPENSE AND RISK.

IF YOU DO MAKE THE GOODS AVAILABLE TO THE SELLER AND THE SELLER DOES NOT PICK THEM UP WITHIN 20 DAYS OF THE DATE OF YOUR NOTICE OF CANCELLATION, YOU MAY RETAIN OR DISPOSE OF THE GOODS WITHOUT ANY FURTHER OBLIGATION. IF YOU FAIL TO MAKE THE GOODS AVAILABLE TO THE SELLER, OR IF YOU AGREE TO RETURN THE GOODS AND FAIL TO DO SO, THEN YOU REMAIN LIABLE FOR PERFORMANCE OF ALL OBLIGATIONS UNDER THE CONTRACT.

TO CANCEL THIS TRANSACTION, MAIL OR DELIVER A SIGNED AND DATED COPY OF THIS CANCELLATION NOTICE OR ANY OTHER WRITTEN NOTICE, OR SEND A TELEGRAM, TO _____[name of seller], AT _____[address of seller's place of business] NOT LATER THAN MIDNIGHT OF _____ (date).

I HEREBY CANCEL THIS TRANSACTION.

_____   _____

(Buyer's signature)   (Date)

The seller must complete the notice and orally inform the buyer of the right to cancel. He cannot misrepresent the right to cancel, assign the contract until the fifth business day, nor include a confession of judgment in the contract. For more specific details see the rules contained in the Code of Federal Regulations, Title 16, Chapter I, Part 429.

MASSACHUSETTS
LAW

Massachusetts also has laws allowing buyers to cancel certain transactions within three days and requiring the seller or lessor to give written notice of this right. Covered transactions are those which are:

- consumer transactions (sales, rental, lease);

- over $25 (including all charges, interest, etc.);

- primarily for personal, family, or household purposes; and,

- consummated other than at the seller's regular place of business.

Right to cancel. Any such sale described above my be canceled by the buyer by written notice postmarked any time before midnight of the third business day after the sales day.

Written agreement. Every such sale must be in writing and must contain the following notice, in bold face type and at least ten point size:

> **You may cancel this agreement if it has been signed by a party thereto at a place other than an address of the seller, which may be his main office or branch thereof, provided you notify the seller in writing at his main office or branch by ordinary mail posted, by telegram sent or by delivery, not later than midnight of the third business day following the signing of this agreement. See the attached notice of cancellation form for an explanation of this right.**

Attached to the notice must be a form in duplicate that is easily detachable, stating the same, in at least ten point boldface type, as the federal notice reproduced on the previous page.

Seller's duty. All businesses conducting solicitation sales must:

- ensure that all employees have the required permits;

- register with the chief of police or other designated official of a town or city; and,

- notify the chief of police or other designated official in each town where sales are to be made.

TELEPHONE SOLICITATION LAWS

Phone calls. Telephone solicitations are governed by the *Telephone Consumer Protection Act* (U.S.C., Title 47, Sec. 227) and the Federal Communications Commission rules implementing the act (C.F.R., Title 47, Sec. 64.1200). Violators of the act can be sued for $500 damages by consumers and can be fined $10,000 by the FCC. Some of the requirements under the law are:

- Calls can only be made between 8 A.M. and 9 P.M.

- Solicitors must keep a "do not call" list and honor requests to not call.

- There must be a written policy that the party called is told the name of the caller; the caller's business name and phone number or address; that the call is a sales call; and the nature of the goods or services.

- Personnel must be trained in the policies.

- Recorded messages cannot be used to call residences.

Faxes. It is illegal under the act to send advertising faxes to anyone who has not consented to receiving such faxes or is an existing customer.

MASSACHUSETTS LAWS

In Massachusetts, with respect to telephone solicitations, the person calling must, before making any other statement except a greeting and before asking any questions, state the identity of the caller, the trade name of the person represented by the caller, and the kind of goods or services being offered for sale. Callers using automatic dialing systems may not call those who have given notice to their telephone company that they do not want to receive those calls.

Automatic dialing. All telephone customers have the right to notify the telephone company that they do not wish to receive telephone calls from an automatic dialing system. The phone company cannot charge for this service.

PRICING, WEIGHTS, AND LABELING

FEDERAL LAW

Food products. Beginning in 1994, all food products were required to have labels with information on the product's nutritional values such as calories, fat, and protein. For most products, the label must be in the required format so that consumers can easily compare products. However, if such a format will not fit on the product label, the information may be in another format which is easily readable.

Metric measures. In 1994, federal rules requiring metric measurement of products took effect. Some federal agencies, such as the federal highway department, indefinitely postponed implementation of the rules, but the Federal Trade Commission (FTC) and the Food and Drug Administration intend to enforce the rules against businesses.

Under these rules, metric measures do not have to be the first measurement on the container, but they must be included. Food items that are packaged as they are sold (such as delicatessen items) do not have to contain metric labels.

MASSACHUSETTS LAW

Massachusetts laws require that every item in food stores and every grocery item in food departments to be individually marked with the correct selling price. Many items are exempted, provided that a conspicuous separate sign indicated the price and that the cashier can readily discern the price of each item.

Massachusetts also has voluminous statutes governing the labeling requirements for a variety of specific items, including the following:

- horse meat;
- potatoes;
- artificial colorings and flavorings;
- preservatives;

- farm products;
- native fruits, vegetables, and turkeys;
- stuffed toys and furniture;
- furs;
- non-original paintings;
- sewing thread;
- poison;
- anti-freeze;
- electric appliances;
- hazardous substances;
- milk cans;
- canned soaked goods;
- honey;
- gold;
- kosher food;
- vinegar;
- prescription drugs;
- alcoholic beverages;
- safety glazing materials;
- explosives;
- cosmetics;
- patent medicine or food; containing drugs;
- frozen desserts;
- baking powder;
- livestock and poultry products;
- lard;
- process or renovated butter;
- imitation butter and cheeses;
- margarine;
- milk and cream;
- bottled water;
- bakery products;
- molasses;
- flammable clothing and fabrics;
- fertilizers;
- seeds;
- shellfish;
- halibut;
- unstable drugs;
- imitation foods; and,
- maple syrup and maple syrup food products.

PAYMENT AND COLLECTION 12

Depending on the business you are in, you may be paid by cash, checks, credit cards, or some sort of financing arrangement such as a promissory note and mortgage. Both state and federal laws affect the type of payments you collect, and failure to follow the laws can cost you considerably.

CASH

Cash is probably the easiest form of payment and it is subject to few restrictions. The most important one is that you keep an accurate accounting of your cash transactions and that you report all of your cash income on your tax return. Recent efforts to stop the drug trade have resulted in some serious penalties for failing to report cash transactions and for money laundering. The laws are so sweeping that even if you deal in cash in an ordinary business, you may violate the law and face huge fines and imprisonment.

The most important law to be concerned with is the one requiring the filing of **IRS FORM 8300** for cash transactions of $10,000 or more. A transaction does not have to happen in one day. If a person brings you smaller amounts of cash that add up to $10,000 and the government can construe them as one transaction, the form must be filed. Under this law, "cash" also includes travelers' checks and money orders, but not cashiers' checks or bank checks. For more information, obtain IRS Form 8300 and instructions from the IRS.

CHECKS

It is important to accept checks in your business. While there is a small percentage that will be bad, most checks will be good, and you will be able to accommodate more customers. To avoid having problems with checks, you should comply with the following rules.

ACCEPTING CHECKS

A business cannot require a customer to provide a credit card number or expiration date in order to pay by check. (Massachusetts General Laws (Mass. Gen. Laws), Chapter (Ch.) 93, Section (Sec.) 105.) The business can request to see a card to establish that the customer is credit-worthy or for additional identification and can record the type of credit card and issuing company. However, the business cannot record the number of the card.

BAD CHECKS

Massachusetts has a fairly effective bad check collection process. If you follow the rules, you may be able to collect on a bad check. Call your local police department to find out how to proceed.

Be sure that you are able to identify the person who gave you the check. To do this, you should require identification and write down the sources of identification on the face of the check. Make sure they sign the check!

REFUNDS AFTER CASHING CHECK

A popular scam is for a person to purchase something by using a check and then come back the next day demanding a refund. After making the refund, the business discovers the initial payment check bounced. Do not make refunds until checks clear!

CREDIT CARDS

In our buy-now, pay-later society, charge cards can add greatly to your sales potential, especially with large, discretionary purchases. For MasterCard, Visa, and Discover, the fees are about two percent, and this amount is easily paid for by the extra purchases that the cards allow. American Express charges four to five percent, and you may decide this is not worth paying since almost everyone who has an American Express card also has another card.

For businesses that have a retail outlet, there is usually no problem getting merchant status. Most commercial banks can handle it. Discover can also set you up to accept their card, as well as MasterCard and Visa, and they will wire the money into your bank account daily.

For mail order businesses, especially those operating out of the home, it is much harder to get merchant status. This is because of the number of scams in which large amounts are charged, no products are shipped, and the company folds. At one point, even a business offering to post a large cash bond and let the bank hold the charges for six months was refused.

Today things are a little better. Some companies are even soliciting merchants. But beware of those that charge exorbitant fees (such as $5 or $10 per order for "processing"). One good thing about American Express is that they will accept mail order companies operating out of the home. However, not as many people have AmEx cards as others.

Some companies open a small storefront (or share one) to get merchant status, then process mostly mail orders. The processors usually do not want to accept you if you will do more than fifty percent mail order; but if you do not have many complaints, you may be allowed to process mostly mail orders. Whatever you do, keep your charge customers happy so that they do not complain!

You might be tempted to try to run your charges through another business. This may be okay if you actually sell your products through them, but if you run your business charges through their account, the other business may lose its merchant status. For example, if you are selling books and running credit card charges through your friend's florist shop account, people who buy a book by mail from you and then have a charge on their credit card statement from a florist shop will probably call the credit card company saying that they never bought anything from the florist shop. Too many of these and your friend's account for her florist shop will be closed.

FINANCING LAWS

Some businesses can make sales more easily if they finance the purchases themselves. If the business has enough capital to do this, it can earn extra profits on the financing terms. Nonetheless, because of abuses, many consumer protection laws have been passed by both the federal and state governments.

FEDERAL LAW

Reg. Z. Two important federal laws regarding financing are called the *Truth in Lending Act* and the *Fair Credit Billing Act*. These are implemented by what is called *Regulation Z* (commonly known as *Reg. Z*), issued by the Board of Governors of the Federal Reserve System. It is contained in Title 12 of the Code of Federal Regulations, page 226. (1 C.F.R., Vol. 12, p. 226.) This is a very complicated law and some have said that no business can be sure to be in compliance with it.

The regulation covers all transactions in which all four of the following conditions are met:

1. credit is offered;

2 the offering of credit is regularly done;

3. there is a finance charge for the credit or there is a written agreement with more than four payments; and,

4. the credit is for personal, family, or household purposes.

It also covers credit card transactions where only the first two conditions above are met. It applies to leases if the consumer ends up paying the full value and keeping the item leased. It does not apply to the following transactions:

- transactions with businesses or agricultural purposes;

- transactions with organizations such as corporations or the government;

- transactions of over $25,000 which are not secured by the consumer's dwelling;

- credit involving public utilities;

- credit involving securities or commodities; and,

- home fuel budget plans.

The way for a small business to avoid Reg. Z violations is to avoid transactions which meet the conditions, or to make sure all transactions fall under the exceptions. This is easy for many businesses. Instead of extending credit to customers, accept credit cards and let the credit card company extend the credit. However, if your customers usually do not have credit cards or if you are in a business, such as used car sales, which often extends credit, you should consult a lawyer knowledgeable about Reg. Z or, if you dare, get a copy for yourself at:

www.cardreport.com/laws/tila/tila.html

MASSACHUSETTS LAW

Massachusetts also has extensive laws regarding financing arrangements. The law governs disclosure, cancellation provisions, and limitations on interest rates. Anyone engaged in installment sales in Massachusetts should carefully review the latest version of Massachusetts General Laws, Chapter 255D, Retail Installment Sales and Services. Chapter 255B, Retail Installment Sales of Motor Vehicles, may also be relevant.

In addition to these acts, Massachusetts forbids discrimination in granting credit based upon age, sex, sexual orientation, marital status, race, color, religion, national origin, children, handicap, or the fact that all or part of one's income comes from an assistance program.

USURY

Usury is the charging of an illegally high rate of interest. In Massachusetts, the maximum rate of interest you may charge is twenty percent, unless you notify the attorney general and keep adequate records (what constitutes adequate records is not explained in the law).

COLLECTIONS

The Fair Debt Collection Practices Act of 1977 bans the use of deception, harassment, and other unreasonable acts in the collection of debts. It has strict requirements whenever someone is collecting a debt for someone else (that is, they do not apply if you are collecting your own debt). If you are in the collection business (i.e., you are in the business of collecting debts owed to others), you must get a copy of this law.

The Federal Trade Commission has issued some rules which prohibit deceptive representations such as pretending to be in the motion picture industry, the government, or a credit bureau, or using questionnaires which do not say that they are for the purpose of collecting a debt. (C.F.R., Title 16, Ch I, Part 237.)

MASSACHUSETTS LAW

The Unfair Debt Collection Practices Law applies to debts owed by persons (not corporations) for transactions which were for personal, family, or household purposes. (Mass. Gen. Law., Ch. 93, Sec. 49.) The law forbids:

- using instruments that simulate judicial process;
- communicating with third parties about the debt without permission of the debtor;
- communicating with the debtor after being notified that communications should be directed to the debtor's attorney; and,
- harassing or embarrassing the debtor.

BUSINESS RELATIONS LAWS 13

THE UNIFORM COMMERCIAL CODE

The *Uniform Commercial Code* is a set of laws regulating numerous aspects of doing business. A national group drafted this set of uniform laws to avoid having a patchwork of different laws around the fifty states. Although some states modified some sections of the laws, the code is basically the same in most of the states. In Massachusetts, the "UCC," as it is called, is contained in chapter 106 of Massachusetts General Laws. Each chapter is concerned with a different aspect of commercial relations such as sales, warranties, bank deposits, commercial paper, and bulk transfers.

Businesses that wish to know their rights in all types of transactions should obtain a copy of the UCC and become familiar with it. It is especially useful in transactions between merchants. However, the meaning is not always clear from a reading of the statutes. In many law schools, students spend a full semester studying each chapter of this law.

COMMERCIAL DISCRIMINATION

FEDERAL LAW

The *Robinson-Patman Act of 1936* prohibits businesses from injuring competition by offering the same goods at different prices to different buyers. This means that the large chain stores should not be getting a better price than your small shop. It also requires that promotional allowances must be made on proportionally the same terms to all buyers.

As a small business, you may be a victim of Robinson-Patman Act violations. A good place to look for information on the act is the following website: **www.lawmall.com/rpa/**.

MASSACHUSETTS LAW

Massachusetts' "Unfair Sales Act" makes unlawful the advertising, offer for sale, and sale of merchandise at less than cost with the "intent to injure competitors or destroy competition."

RESTRAINING TRADE

FEDERAL LAW

One of the earliest federal laws affecting business is the *Sherman Antitrust Act of 1890*. The purpose of the law was to protect competition in the marketplace by prohibiting monopolies. For example, one large company might buy out all of its competitors and then raise prices to astronomical levels. In recent years, this law was used to break up AT&T.

Examples of some things that are prohibited are:

- agreements between competitors to sell at the same prices;
- agreements between competitors on how much will be sold or produced;
- agreements between competitors to divide up a market;
- refusing to sell one product without a second product; and,
- exchanging information among competitors which results in similarity of prices.

As a new business, you probably will not be in a position to violate the act, but you should be aware of it in case a larger competitor tries to put you out of business. A good place to find information on the act is at: **www.lawmall.com/sherman.act/index.html**.

MASSACHUSETTS LAW

Massachusetts anti-trust laws are substantially identical to federal laws. Where federal laws do not apply because interstate commerce is not involved, the Massachusetts laws would apply to business activities in Massachusetts.

INTELLECTUAL PROPERTY PROTECTION

As a business owner, you should know enough about intellectual property law to protect your own creations and to keep from violating the rights of others. Intellectual property is that which is the product of human creativity, such as writings, designs, inventions, melodies, and processes. They are things which can be stolen without being physically taken. For example, if you write a book, someone can steal the words from your book without stealing a physical copy of it.

As the Internet grows, intellectual property is becoming more valuable. Smart business owners are those who will take the action necessary to protect their company's intellectual property. Additionally, business owners should know intellectual property law to be sure that they do not violate the rights of others. Even an unknowing violation of the law can result in stiff fines and penalties.

The following are the types of intellectual property and the ways to protect them.

PATENT

A *patent* is protection given to new and useful inventions, discoveries, and designs. To be entitled to a patent, a work must be completely new and "unobvious." A patent is granted to the first inventor who files for the patent. Once an invention is patented, no one else can make use of that invention, even if they discover it independently after a lifetime of research. A patent protects an invention for seventeen years and protects designs for three-and-a-half, seven, or fourteen years. Patents cannot be renewed. The patent application must clearly explain how to make the invention so that when the patent expires, others will be able to freely make and use the invention. Patents are registered with the United States Patent and Trademark Office (USPTO). Examples of things which would be patentable would be mechanical devices or new drug formulas.

COPYRIGHT

A *copyright* is protection given to "original works of authorship," such as written works, musical works, visual works, performance works, or computer software programs. A copyright exists from the moment of creation, but one cannot register a copyright until it has been fixed in tangible form. Also, one cannot copyright titles, names, or slogans. A copyright currently gives the author and his heirs exclusive right to his work for the life of the author plus seventy years. Copyrights first registered before 1978 last for ninety-five years. This was previously seventy-five years but was extended twenty years to match the European system. Copyrights are registered with the Register of Copyrights at the Library of Congress. Examples of works that would be copyrightable are books, paintings, songs, poems, plays, drawings, and films.

TRADEMARK

A *trademark* is protection given to a name or symbol which is used to distinguish one person's goods or services from those of others. It can consist of letters, numerals, packaging, labeling, musical notes, colors, or a combination of these. If a trademark is used on services, as opposed to goods, it is called a *service mark*. A trademark lasts indefinitely if it is used continuously and renewed properly. Trademarks are registered with the United States Patent and Trademark Office and with individual states. This is explained further in Chapter 3. Examples of trademarks are the "Chrysler" name on automobiles, the red border on TIME magazine, and the shape of the Coca-Cola bottle.

TRADE SECRETS

A *trade secret* is some information or process that provides a commercial advantage, which is protected by keeping it a secret. Examples of trade secrets may be a list of successful distributors, the formula for Coca-Cola, or some unique source code in a computer program. Trade secrets are not registered anywhere, but are protected by the fact that they are not disclosed. They are protected only for as long as they are kept secret. If you independently discover the formula for Coca-Cola tomorrow, you can freely market it. (But you cannot use the trademark "Coca-Cola" on your product to market it.)

Massachusetts law. Massachusetts law provides that stealing trade secrets constitutes larceny. Penalties include fines of up to $25,000 and/or imprisonment.

NON-PROTECTABLE CREATIONS

Some things are just not protectable. Such things as ideas, systems, and discoveries are not allowed any protection under any law. If you have a great idea, such as selling packets of hangover medicine in bars, you cannot stop others from doing the same thing. If you invent a new medicine, you can patent it; if you pick a distinctive name for it, you can register it as a trademark; if you create a unique picture or instructions for the package, you can copyright them. You cannot stop others from using your basic business idea of marketing hangover medicine in bars.

Notice the subtle differences between the protective systems available. If you invent something two days after someone else does, you cannot even use it yourself if the other person has patented it. But if you write the same poem as someone else and neither of you copied the other, both of you can copyright the poem. If you patent something, you can have the exclusive rights to it for the term of the patent, but you must disclose how others can make it after the patent expires. However, if you keep it a trade secret, you have exclusive rights as long as no one learns the secret.

We are in a time of transition of the law of intellectual property. New changes are made in the laws and new forms of creativity win protection every year. For more information, you should consult a new edition of a book on these types of property. Some are listed in the section of this book titled "For Further Reference."

ENDLESS LAWS 14

The Commonwealth of Massachusetts and the federal government have numerous laws and rules which apply to every aspect of every type of business. There are laws governing even such things as exploding golf balls and selling baby food at flea markets.

Some activities are covered by both state and federal laws. In such cases, you must obey the stricter of the rules. In addition, more than one agency of the state or federal government may have rules governing your business. Each of these may have the power to investigate violations and impose fines or other penalties.

Penalties for violations of these laws can range from a warning to a criminal fine and even jail time. In some cases, employees can sue for damages. Recently, employees have been given awards of millions of dollars from employers who violated the law. Since "ignorance of the law is no excuse," it is your duty to learn which laws apply to your business or to risk these penalties.

Very few people in business know the laws that apply to their businesses. If you take the time to learn them, you can become an expert in your field, and avoid problems with regulators. You can also fight back if one of your competitors uses some illegal method to compete with you.

The laws and rules which affect the most businesses are explained in this section. Following that is a list of more specialized laws. You should read through this list and see which ones may apply to your business. Then go to your public library or law library and read them. Some may not apply to your phase of the business, but if any of them do apply, you should make copies to keep on hand.

No one could possibly know all the rules that affect business, much less comply with them all. The Interstate Commerce Commission alone has forty trillion (that is forty million million or 40,000,000,000,000) rates on its books telling the transportation industry what it should charge! But if you keep up with the important rules, you will stay out of trouble and have more chance of success.

FEDERAL LAWS

The federal laws which are most likely to affect small businesses are rules of the Federal Trade Commission (FTC). The FTC has some rules which affect many businesses such as the rules about labeling, warranties, and mail order sales. Other rules affect only certain industries.

If you sell goods by mail, you should send for their booklet, *A Business Guide to the Federal Trade Commission's Mail Order Rule*. If you are going to be involved in a certain industry, such as those listed below, or using warranties or your own labeling, you should ask for their latest information on the subject. The address is:

Federal Trade Commission
Washington, DC 20580

The rules of the FTC are contained in the Code of Federal Regulations (CFR) in Chapter 16. Some of the industries covered are:

INDUSTRY	PART
Adhesive Compositions	235
Aerosol Products Used for Frosting Cocktail Glasses	417

INDUSTRY	PART
Automobiles (New car fuel economy advertising)	259
Barber Equipment and Supplies	248
Binoculars	402
Business Opportunities and Franchises	436
Cigarettes	408
Decorative Wall Paneling	243
Dog and Cat Food	241
Dry Cell Batteries	403
Extension Ladders	418
Fallout Shelters	229
Feather and Down Products	253
Fiber Glass Curtains	413
Food (Games of Chance)	419
Funerals	453
Gasoline (Octane posting)	306
Gasoline	419
Greeting Cards	244
Home Entertainment Amplifiers	432
Home Insulation	460
Hosiery	22
Household Furniture	250
Jewelry	23
Ladies' Handbags	247
Law Books	256
Light Bulbs	409
Luggage and Related Products	24
Mail Order Insurance	234
Mail Order Merchandise	435
Men's and Boys' Tailored Clothing	412
Metallic Watch Band	19

INDUSTRY	PART
Mirrors	21
Nursery	18
Ophthalmic Practices	456
Photographic Film and Film Processing	242
Private Vocational and Home Study Schools	254
Radiation Monitoring Instruments	232
Retail Food Stores (Advertising)	424
Shell Homes	230
Shoes	231
Sleeping Bags	400
Tablecloths and Related Products	404
Television Sets	410
Textile Wearing Apparel	423
Textiles	236
Tires	228
Used Automobile Parts	20
Used Lubricating Oil	406
Used Motor Vehicles	455
Waist Belts	405
Watches	245
Wigs and Hairpieces	252

Some other federal laws which affect businesses are as follows:

- Alcohol Administration Act (U.S.C., Title 29, beginning with Sec. 201)

- Child Protection and Toy Safety Act (1969)

- Clean Water Act (U.S.C., Title 33)

- Comprehensive Smokeless Tobacco Health Education Act (1986) See also C.F.R., Title 16, Ch. I, Part 307 for rules.

- Consumer Credit Protection Act (1968)

- Consumer Product Safety Act (1972)

- Energy Policy and Conservation Act. See also C.F.R., Title 16, Ch. I, Part 305 for rules about energy cost labeling

- Environmental Pesticide Control Act of 1972

- Fair Credit Reporting Act (1970)

- Fair Packaging and Labeling Act (1966). See also C.F.R., Title 16, Ch. I, Parts 500-503 for rules

- Flammable Fabrics Act (1953). See also C.F.R., Title 16, Ch. II, Parts 1602–1632 for rules

- Food, Drug, and Cosmetic Act (U.S.C., Title 21, beginning with Sec. 301)

- Fur Products Labeling Act (1951). See also C.F.R., Title 16, Ch. I, Part 301 for rules

- Hazardous Substances Act (1960)

- Hobby Protection Act. See also C.F.R., Title 16, Ch. I, Part 304 for rules

- Insecticide, Fungicide, and Rodenticide Act (U.S.C., Title 7, beginning with Sec. 136)

- Magnuson-Moss Warranty Act. See C.F.R., Title 16, Ch. I, Part 239 for rules

- Poison Prevention Packaging Act of 1970. See also C.F.R., Title 16, Ch. II, Parts 1700-1702 for rules

- Solid Waste Disposal Act (U.S.C., Title 42, beginning with Sec. 6901)

- Textile Fiber Products Identification Act. See also C.F.R., Title 16, Ch. I, Part 303 for rules

- Toxic Substance Control Act (U.S.C., Title 15)

- Wool Products Labeling Act (1939). See also C.F.R., Title 16, Ch. I, Part 300 for rules

- Nutrition Labeling and Education Act of 1990. See also C.F.R., Title 21, Ch. 1, Subchapter. B

- Food Safety Enforcement Enhancement Act of 1997

Massachusetts Laws

Massachusetts has numerous laws regulating specific types of businesses or certain activities of businesses. The following is a list of those laws that are most likely to affect small businesses. If you are running a type of business which is not mentioned here, or using some sales technique which could come under government regulation, you should check the indexes to the Massachusetts General Laws and the Massachusetts Code of Regulations. Since these indexes are not well done, you should look up every possible synonym or related word to be sure not to miss anything. You can find the laws online at **www.state.ma.us/legis /laws/mgl/index.htm** (not an official version, but fairly accurate nonetheless).

Citations refer to Massachusetts General Laws (Mass. Gen. Laws). If no sections are cited, the entire chapter cited applies.

	Chapter(s)	Section(s)
Acupuncturists	112	148-162
Adoption Agencies	210	
Adulteration and misbranding of food and drugs	94	185-196
Agents, consignees and factors	104	
Agricultural and other seeds	128	84-101
Alcoholic liquors	138	
Allied mental health and human services professionals	112	163-172
Ambulances and EMTs	111C	
Anti-freeze solutions	94	303G-303M
Antitrust act	93	
Apples	94	100-105
	128	102-115
Architects	112	60A-60O
Assignment of wages	154	
Athletic trainers	112	23F
Auctioneers	100	

Chapter(s)	Section(s)	
Audiologists	112	138-147
Bakeries and bakery products .	94	2-10
Baking powder	94	2-10
Bank deposits and collections	106	4-101-4-504
Barbers	112	87F-87S
Bells, whistles and gongs	149	175
Brokers	112	87UU
Butter, cheese and lard	94	49-63
Cancelation of agreements	93	48-48A
Canned goods and molasses	94	154-156
Carriers of property by motor vehicle	159B	
Cemeteries	114	
Certain business corporations	156B	
Certified health officers	112	87WWW-87ZZZ
Certified public accountants	112	87A-87E ½
Chiropractors	112	89-97
Cinematographers operating in public buildings	143	75
Clinical laboratories	111D	
Coal, coke, charcoal and kindling wood	94	238-249F
Cold storage	94	66-73
Collection agencies	93	24-28
Commercial drivers	90F	
Commercial feeds	128	51-63
Commercial fertilizers	128	64-83
Commercial paper	106	3-101-3-805
Consignment of fine art	104A	
Consumer credit reporting	93	50-68
Consumer privacy in commercial transactions	93	104, 105
Cosmetologists	112	87T-87KK
Cranberries	94	115-117
Credit services organizations	93	68A-68E
Credit slips	93	14S
Day care providers	28A	

	Chapter(s)	Section(s)
Debt collection	93	49
Demonstration sheep farms	128	9-11
Dentists	112	43-53
Discrimination against handicapped persons	93	102, 103
Discrimination based on race, color, religious creed, national origin, ancestry, or sex	151B	
Discrimination in employment on account of age	149	24A-24J
Discriminatory wage rates based on sex	149	105A-105C
Dishonored checks	93	40A
Dispensing opticians	112	73C-73M
Eggs	94	89-92A
Electric appliances	94	314-318
Electricians	141	
Electrologists	112	87EEE-87OOO
Embalmers and funeral directors	112	82-87
Emergency medical care	111C	
Employment of aliens	149	19C
Engineers	112	81D-81T
Enrichment of bread and flour	94	10H-10K
Equipment dealers	93G	
False advertisement for help or employment	149	21
Farm products	94	117A-117F
Fish	94	77A-88D
Foresters	132	47-50
Frozen desserts and frozen dessert mix	94	65G-65U
Frozen food	94	73A
Fruits, vegetables and nuts	94	96-99B
Fuel oils	94	303F
Furs	94	277A
Gasoline dealers	93E	1-9
Grain and meal	94	219-224
Hay	94	236
Hazardous substances	94B	

	Chapter(s)	Section(s)
Hazardous substances disclosure by employers	111F	
Hazardous waste site cleanup professionals	21A	19C
Health and safety	149	106-142
Health clubs	93	78-88
Hearing aids	93	71-75
Heating oils	94	249H
Herring, alewives, etc.	130	93-96
Home improvement contractors	142A	
Horse and dog racing meetings	128A	
Hospitals, clinics and dispensaries	111	50-57D
Ice	94	157-162
Imported goods	94	277B
Inland fisheries and game	131	
Inspection and sale of meat	94	146-153A
Insurance agents	175	
Insurance premium finance agencies	255C	
Junkyards	140B	
Kennel operators	140	137A
Kosher foods	94	156
Labels, trademarks and trade names	110	
Land surveyors	112	81D-81T
Landscape architects	112	98-107
Laundries and dry cleaning establishments	93	18A, 18B
Liability of employers to employees for injuries not resulting in a death	153	
Lime and lime casks	94	262-268
Limited partnerships	109	
Lobsters	130	37-51A
Manufacturers and sellers of upholstered furniture, bedding, or stuffed toys or filling for same	94	271
Maple syrup and maple syrup food products	128	36C
Marine fish and fisheries	130	
Marking of packages containing food	94	181-184E

	Chapter(s)	Section(s)
Maternity leave	149	105D
Measurement of lumber	96	
Measuring of leather	95	
Meats, poultry, and fish	94	92B
Methyl or wood alcohol	94	303A-303E
Milk and cream	94	12-48D
Milk control	94A	
Minimum fair wages	151	
Mining stocks	93	15-18
Mortgage transactions	93	70
Motion picture distributors	93F	1-4
Motor vehicle damage repair shops	100A	
Motor vehicle manufacturers, distributors, and dealers	93B	1-15
Multi-level distribution companies	93	69
Nails	94	278-282
Noisome trades	111	143-154
Non-alcoholic beverages	94	10A-10G
Nuisances	111	122-131
Nurses	112	74-81C
Nursing home administrators	112	108-117
Nursing homes	93	76
Occupational therapists	112	23G
Occupational therapy assistants	112	23H
Operators of drinking water supply facilities	112	87CCCC-87DDDD
Operators of hoisting machinery not run by stead	146	53-55
Operators of security systems businesses	147	57-61
Optometrists	112	66-73B
Outdoor advertising adjacent to interstate and primary highway systems	93D	1-7
Outdoor advertising signs and devices within public view	93	29-33
Paintings	94	277C

	Chapter(s)	Section(s)
Partnerships	108A	
Pesticides	132B	
Petroleum products	94	295A-295W
Pharmacists	112	24-36
Physical therapists	112	23J
Physical therapy assistants	112	23J
Physicians and surgeons	112	2-9B, 10-12CC
Physicians assistants	112	9C-9K
Pick-your-own farming operations	128	2E
Pilots	103	
Plant closings	151A	71A-71H
Plumbers	142	
Podiatrists	112	13-22
Potatoes	94	117G-117L
Professional corporations	156A	
Prohibition of certain discrimination by businesses	151E	
Psychologists	112	118-137
Public warehouses	105	
Radio and television technicians	112	87PPP-87VVV
Real estate brokers and salesmen	112	87PP-87DDD½
Real estate appraisers	112	173-195
Registration and protection of trademarks	110B	
Regulation of business practices for consumers protection	93A	1-11
Removal, termination or fire sales	93	28A-28F
Rental agreements for personal property used primarily for household or family use	93	90-94
Research institutions using dogs or cats for experimentation	140	174D
Respiratory therapists	112	23R-23BB
Retail clothing stores dressing room surveillance	93	89
Retail drug stores	112	37-42A
Retail trade reporting agencies	93	49A

	Chapter(s)	Section(s)
Sales	106	2-101--2-725
Sales by weight	94	176-180
Sales financiers	255B	2
Sanitarians	112	87LL-87OO
Sausages	94	142-143A
Scallops	130	92
School bus operators	90	8-8A 1/2
Secured transactions	106	9-101--9-507
Self-service storage facilities	105A	
Sellers of ammunitions	140	122B
Sellers of milk or cream to other than consumers	94	41A
Shellfish	130	52-75
Shipping and seamen	102	1-4
Slaughter houses	94	118-139G
Slot machines	94	283, 284
Social workers	112	130-137
Solicitation of business on public sidewalks	93	40
Speech language pathologists	112	138-147
Stables	111	155-158
	128	2B
Striped bass	130	100A-100B
Surveying of land	97	
Taking of trade secrets	93	42
Tanning facilities	111	207-214
Thread	94	285-288
Timothy or herdsgrass seed	94	237
Trade schools	93	20A-21G
Trading stamp companies	93	14L-14R
Transient vendors, hawkers, and peddlers	101	
Turpentine, paints, and linseed oil	94	289-295
Unemployment benefits	151A	22-37
Unemployment compensation contributions	151A	13-21
Unfair sales	93	14E-14K

	Chapter(s)	Section(s)
Unsolicited merchandise	93	43
Upholstered furniture, bedding, and stuffed toys	94	270-277
Vending machines	94	308-313
Veterinarians	112	54-60
Victuallers and innkeepers	140	2-21
Video rentals	93	106
Vinegar	94	163-171
Waiver of consumer rights	93	101
Warehouse receipts, bills of lading, other documents of title	106	7-101-7-603
Weekly payment of wages	149	148-159B
Weighers of beef	94	140-141
Weights and measures	98	
Wholesale food processing and distribution	94	305C
Wholesale sale, distribution or delivery of drugs or medicines	112	36A-36D
Wood and bark	94	296-303
Workers' compensation	152	

YOUR BUSINESS AND THE INTERNET 15

The Internet has opened up a world of opportunities for businesses. A few years ago, getting national visibility cost a fortune. Today a business can set up a Web page for a few hundred dollars and, with some clever publicity and a little luck, millions of people around the world will see it.

But this new world has new legal issues and new liabilities. Not all of them have been addressed by laws or by the courts. Before you begin doing business on the Internet, you should know the existing rules and the areas where legal issues exist.

DOMAIN NAMES

CHOOSING AND REGISTERING YOUR DOMAIN NAME

If your business will have a website, you will need to choose and register a domain name. A domain name is the name by which people identify and locate your website, such as **www.SphinxLegal.com**. A company often uses the main part of its name as its domain name. You also might consider a domain name that describes what you are selling, how you are selling it, or something along those lines. To check on whether a domain name is available, go to **www.internic.net/whois.html** or **www.netsol.com/cgi-bin/whois/whois** and follow the directions. The latter site is the site of VeriSign, which used to be Network Solutions, Inc., which was the first and only domain name registrar. Now there are scores of registrars through which you can register a domain name. For a list of accredited domain name registrars, go to:

www.internic.net/regist.html.

Once you choose a domain name and determine that it's not already taken, you are ready to register the name. You don't need to have a site created or hosted in order to register the name. Just call or go to the website of an accredited domain name registrar and follow the directions. Be sure to print out any necessary instructions, and remember your password! When you register your domain name you will need to give contact and technical information. If you don't have a host yet for your website, or you don't know the information for your host, the registrar will provide some temporary host information which you will need to change later.

CYBERSQUATTING You may come up with a great domain name that may be owned by a *cybersquatter*. You may be able to take the name away from that owner under the Uniform Dispute Resolution Policy (the UDRP) of ICANN (Internet Corporation for Assigned Names and Numbers), which is a non-profit corporation that manages the Internet domain name system. Madonna was successful in taking the domain name **www.madonna.com** away from a cybersquatter under the UDRP. You can read the policy at **www.icann.org/dndr/udrp/policy.htm**.

Arbitration is required to commence a dispute, and the cost is primarily the complainant's. To succeed in a dispute under the UDRP, the complainant must show three things:

- that the domain name is identical or confusingly similar to a trademark or service mark in which the complainant has rights;

- that the domain name registrant has no rights or legitimate interests in respect of the domain name; and,

- that the domain name has been registered and is being used in bad faith.

The first element is self-explanatory. As for the second, the policy sets forth some factors which are considered in determining whether a registrant has rights or legitimate interests in a domain name, including use of the name in a bona fide offering of goods or services, whether the registrant has been commonly known by the domain name, and whether the registrant is making a legitimate noncommercial or fair use of the domain name without intent to obtain commercial gain by misleadingly diverting consumers or tarnishing the mark in issue. Other factors may also be considered in determining whether the second element exists.

The third element, the question of bad faith, is probably the most controversial and complicated. The UDRP provides for four nonexclusive circumstances which, if shown, will prove bad faith:

- if the domain name was registered or acquired primarily for the purpose of selling, renting or otherwise transferring the domain name registration to the trademark owner or its competitor for valuable consideration in excess of the costs directly related to registering or acquiring the domain name;

- if the domain name was registered in order to prevent the trademark owner from using it as a domain name, provided that the domain name registrant has engaged in a pattern of such conduct;

- if the domain name was registered for the purpose of disrupting the business of a competitor; or,

- if the domain name registrant has used the domain name to intentionally attempt to attract, for commercial gain, Internet users to its website, by creating a likelihood of confusion with the trademark as to the source, sponsorship, affiliation, or endorsement of the website or of a product or service on the website.

The UDRP provides that the arbitrators may order the cancellation or transfer to the complainant of the domain name. An appeal process is also provided for.

There is a corresponding federal law, the *Anticybersquatting Consumer Protection Act*, which provides for liability of a cybersquatter to a trademark owner if the person acts in bad faith to profit from the trademark and registers, traffics in, or abuses a domain name that is either identical or confusingly similar to a distinctive mark, or is identical, confusingly similar, or dilutive of a famous mark. The Act provides for proceedings where an action can be filed against the domain name in the district where the domain name registrar is located, when the defendant cannot be located. The remedy to be obtained in this type of proceeding is limited to the transfer of the domain name or forfeiture or cancellation of the trademark. In a proceeding where a trademark owner personally sues the domain name owner, money damages can be obtained as well.

To protect your domain name, you may want to register it as a trademark. To do this, the name would have to be used to describe the goods or services or services you are selling. Chapter 3 contains some basic information about trademarks.

WEB PAGES

There are many new companies eager to help you set up a website. Some offer turnkey sites for a low flat rate. Custom sites can cost tens of thousands of dollars. If you have plenty of capital you may want to have your site handled by one of these professionals. However, setting up a website is a fairly simple process, and once you learn the basics you can handle most of it in-house.

If you are new to the Web, you may want to look at the following sites, which will familiarize you with the Internet jargon and give you a basic introduction to the Web:

www.learnthenet.com   www.webopedia.com

SITE SETUP   There are seven steps to setting up a website: site purpose, design, content, structure, programming, testing, and publicity. Whether you do it yourself, hire a professional site designer, or use a college student, the steps toward creating an effective site are the same.

Before beginning your own site you should look at other sites, including those of major corporations and of small businesses. Look at the sites of all the companies that compete with you. Look at hundreds of sites and click through them to see how they work (or do not work).

Site purpose. To know what to include on your site, you must decide what its purpose will be. Do you want to take orders for your products or services, attract new employees, give away samples, or show off your company headquarters? You might want to do several of these things.

Site design. After looking at other sites you can see that there are numerous ways to design a site. It can be crowded, or open and airy; it can have several windows (frames) open at once or just one, and it can allow long scrolling or just click-throughs.

You will have to decide whether the site will have text only; text plus photographs and graphics; or text plus photos, graphics, and other design elements such as animation or Java script. Additionally, you will begin to make decisions about colors, fonts, and the basic graphic appearance of the site.

Site content. You must create the content for your site. For this, you can use your existing promotional materials, you can write new material just for the website, or you can use a combination of the two. Whatever you choose, remember that the written material should be concise, free of errors, and easy for your target audience to read. Any graphics, including photographs, and written materials not created by you require permission. You should obtain such permission from the lawful copyright holder in order to use any copyrighted material. Once you know your site's purpose, look, and content, you can begin to piece the site together.

Site structure. You must decide how the content (text plus photographs, graphics, animation, etc.) will be structured (what content will be on which page), and how a user will link from one part of the site to another. For example, your first page may have the business name and then choices to click on, such as "about us," "opportunities," "product catalog," etc. Have those choices connect to another page containing the detailed information so that a user will see the catalog when they click on "product catalog." Or your site could have a choice to click on a link to another website related to yours.

Site programming and setup. When you know nothing about setting up a website, it can seem like a daunting task that will require an expert. However, *programming* here means merely putting a site together. There are inexpensive computer programs available that make it very simple.

Commercial programs such as Microsoft FrontPage, Dreamweaver, Pagemaker, Photoshop, MS Publisher, and PageMill allow you to set up Web pages as easily as laying out a print publication. These programs will convert the text and graphics you create into HTML, the programming language of the Web. Before you choose Web design software and design your site, you should determine which Web hosting service you will use. Make sure that the design software you use is compatible with the host server's system. The Web host will be the provider who will give you space on their server and who may provide other services to you, such as secure order processing and analysis of your site to see who is visiting and linking to it.

If you have an America Online account, you can download design software and a tutorial for free. AOL has recently collaborated with a Web hosting service at **www.verioprimehost.com** and offers a number of different hosting packages for the consumer and e-business. You do not have to use AOL's design software in order to use this service. You are eligible to use this site whether you design your own pages, have someone else do the design work for you, or use AOL's templates. This service allows you to use your own domain name and choose the package that is appropriate for your business.

If you have used a page layout program, you can usually get a simple Web page up and running within a day or two. If you do not have much experience with a computer, you might consider hiring a college student to set up a Web page for you.

Site testing. Some of the website setup programs allow you to thoroughly check your new site to see if all the pictures are included and all the links are proper. There are also websites you can go to that will check out your site. Some even allow you to improve your site, such as by reducing the size of your graphics so they download faster. Use a major search engine like the ones listed below to look for companies that can test your site before you launch it on the Web.

Site publicity. Once you set up your website, you will want to get people to look at it. *Publicity* means getting your site noticed as much as possible by drawing people to it.

The first thing to do to get noticed is to be sure your site is registered with as many *search engines* as possible. These are pages that people use to find things on the Internet, such as Yahoo and Excite. They do not automatically know about you just because you created a website. You must tell them about your site, and they must examine and catalog it.

For a fee, there are services that will register your site with numerous search engines. If you are starting out on a shoestring, you can easily do it yourself. While there are hundreds of search engines, most people use a dozen or so of the bigger ones. If your site is in a niche area, such as geneology services, then you would want to be listed on any specific geneology search engines. Most businesses should be mainly concerned with getting on the biggest ones. The biggest search engines at this time are:

search.msn.com	www.hotbot.com
www.about.com	www.infoseek.com
www.askjeeves.com	www.looksmart.com
www.altavista.com	www.lycos.com
www.excite.com	www.metacrawler.com
www.fastsearch.com	www.webcrawler.com
www.google.com	www.yahoo.com

Most of these sites have a place to click to "add your site" to their system. There are sites that rate the search engines, help you list on the search engines, or check to see if you are listed. One site is:

www.searchiq.com

A *meta tag* is an invisible subject word added to your site that can be found by a search engine. For example, if you are a pest control company, you may want to list all of the scientific names of the pests you control and all of the treatments you have available; but you may not need them to be part of the visual design of your site. List these words as meta tags when you set up your page so people searching for those words will find your site.

Some companies thought that a clever way to get viewers would be to use commonly searched names, or names of major competitors, as meta tags to attract people looking for those big companies. For example, a small delivery service that has nothing to do with UPS or Federal Express might use those company names as meta tags so people looking for them would find the smaller company. While it may sound like a good idea, it has been declared illegal trademark infringement. Today many companies have computer programs scanning the Internet for improper use of their trademarks.

ADVERTISING Once you have made sure that your site is passively listed in all the search engines, you may want to actively promote your site. However, self-promotion is seen as a bad thing on the Internet, especially if its purpose is to make money.

Newsgroups are places on the Internet where people interested in a specific topic can exchange information. For example, expectant mothers have a group where they can trade advice and experiences. If you have a product that would be great for expectant mothers, that would be a good place for it to be discussed. However, if you log into the group and merely announce your product, suggesting people order it from your website, you will probably be *flamed* (sent a lot of hate mail).

If you join the group, however, and become a regular, and in answer to someone's problem, mention that you "saw this product that might help," your information will be better received. It may seem unethical to plug your product without disclosing your interest, but this is a procedure used by many large companies. They hire people to plug their product (or rock star) all over the Internet. So, perhaps it has become an acceptable marketing method and consumers know to take plugs with a grain of salt. Let your conscience be your guide.

Keep in mind that Internet publicity works both ways. If you have a great product and people love it, you will get a lot of business. If you sell a shoddy product, give poor service, and do not keep your customers happy, bad publicity on the Internet can kill your business. Besides being an equalizer between large and small companies, the Internet can be a filtering mechanism between good and bad products.

There is no worse breach of Internet etiquette ("netiquette") than to send advertising by e-mail to strangers. It is called *spamming*, and doing it can have serious consequences. There is anti-spamming legislation currently pending at the federal level. Many states, including California, Colorado, Connecticut, Delaware, Idaho, Illinois, Iowa, Louisiana, Missouri, Nevada, North Carolina, Oklahoma, Pennsylvania, Rhode Island, Tennessee, Virginia, Washington, and West Virginia, have enacted anti-spamming legislation. This legislation sets specific requirements for unsolicited bulk e-mail and makes certain practices illegal. You should check with an attorney to see if your business practices fall within the legal limits of these laws. Additionally, many Internet Service Providers (ISPs) have restrictions on unsolicited bulk e-mail (spam); you should check with your ISP to make sure you do not violate its policies.

Banner ads are the small rectangular ads on many Web pages that usually blink or move. Although most computer users seem to have become immune to them, there is still a big market in the sale and exchange of them.

If your site gets enough viewers, people may pay you to place their ads there. Another possibility is to trade ads with another site. In fact there are companies that broker ad trades among websites. Such trades used to be taxable transactions, but after January 5, 2000, such trades are no longer taxable under IRS Notice 2000-6.

LEGAL ISSUES

Before you set up a Web page, you should consider the legal issues described below.

Jurisdiction is the power of a court in a particular location to decide a particular case. Usually you have to have been physically present in a jurisdiction or have done business there before you can be sued there. Since the Internet extends your business's ability to reach people in far-away places, there may be instances when you could be subject to legal jurisdiction far from your own state (or country). There are a number of cases that have been decided in this country regarding the Internet and jurisdiction, but very few cases have been decided on this issue outside of the United States.

In most instances, U.S. courts use the pre-Internet test—whether you have been present in another jurisdiction or have had enough contact with someone in the other jurisdiction. The fact that the Internet itself is not a "place" will not shield you from being sued in another state when you have shipped you company's product there, have entered into a contract with a resident of that state, or have defamed a foreign resident with content on your website.

According to the Court, there is a spectrum of contact required between you, your website, and consumers or audiences. (*Zippo Manufacturing Co. v. Zippo Dot Com, Inc.*, 952 F. Supp. 1119 (W.D. Pa 1997)) It is *clear* that the one end of the spectrum includes the shipping, contracting, and defamation mentioned above as sufficient to establish jurisdiction. The more interactive your site is with consumers, the more you target an audience for your goods in a particular location, and the farther you reach to send your goods out into the world; the more it becomes possible for someone to sue you outside of your own jurisdiction—possibly even in another country.

The law is not even remotely final on these issues. The American Bar Association, among other groups, is studying this topic in detail. At present, no final, global solution or agreement about jurisdictional issues exists.

One way to protect yourself from the possibility of being sued in a far-away jurisdiction would be to have a statement on your website stating that those using the site or doing business with you agree that "jurisdiction for any actions regarding this site" or your company will be in your home county.

For extra protection you can have a preliminary page that must be clicked before entering your website. However, this may be overkill for a small business with little risk of lawsuits. If you are in any business for which you could have serious liability, you should review some competitors' sites and see how they handle the liability issue. They often have a place to click for "legal notice" or "disclaimer" on their first page.

You may want to consult with an attorney to discuss the specific disclaimer you will use on your website, where it should appear, and whether you will have users of your site actively agree to this disclaimer or just passively read it. However, these disclaimers are not enforceable everywhere in the world. Until there is global agreement on jurisdictional issues, this may remain an area of uncertainty for some time to come.

LIBEL *Libel* is any publication that injures the reputation of another. This can occur in print, writing, pictures, or signs. All that is required for *publication* is that you transmit the material to at least one other person. When putting together your website you must keep in mind that it is visible to millions of people all over the planet and that if you libel a person or company you may have to pay damages. Many countries do not have the freedom of speech that we do and a statement that is not libel in the United States may be libelous elsewhere.

COPYRIGHT INFRINGEMENT It is so easy to copy and borrow information on the Internet that it is easy to infringe copyrights without even knowing it. A *copyright* exists for a work as soon as the creator creates it. There is no need to register the copyright or to put a copyright notice on it. So, practically everything on the Internet belongs to someone. Some people freely give their works away. For example, many people have created web artwork (*gifs* and *animated gifs*) that they freely allow people to copy. There are numerous sites that provide hundreds or thousands of free gifs that you can add to your Web pages. Some require you to acknowledge the source; some do not.

You should always be sure that the works are free for the taking before using them.

LINKING AND FRAMING

One way to violate copyright laws is to improperly link other sites to yours either directly or with framing. *Linking* is when you provide a place on your site to click, which takes someone to another site. *Framing* occurs when you set up your site so that when you link to another site, your site is still viewable as a frame around the linked-to site.

While many sites are glad to be linked to others, some, especially providers of valuable information, object. Courts have ruled that linking and framing can be a copyright violation. One rule that has developed is that it is usually okay to link to the first page of a site, but not to link to some valuable information deeper within the site. The rationale for this is that the owner of the site wants visitors to go through the various levels of his or her site (viewing all the ads) before getting the information. By linking directly to the information, you are giving away their product without the ads.

The problem with linking to the first page of a site is that it may be a tedious or difficult task to find the needed page from there. Many sites are poorly designed and make it nearly impossible to find anything.

The best solution, if you wish to link to another page, is to ask permission. Email the Webmaster or other person in charge of the site, if one is given, and explain what you want to do. If they grant permission, be sure to print out a copy of their e-mail for your records.

PRIVACY

Since the Internet is such an easy way to share information, there are many concerns that it will cause a loss of individual privacy. The two main concerns arise when you post information that others consider private, and when you gather information from customers and use it in a way that violates their privacy.

While public actions of politicians and celebrities are fair game, details about their private lives are sometimes protected by law, and details about persons who are not public figures are often protected. The laws in each state are different, and what might be allowable in one state could be illegal in another. If your site will provide any personal information about individuals, you should discuss the possibility of liability with an attorney.

Several well-known companies have been in the news lately for violations of their customers' privacy. They either shared what the customer was buying or downloading, or looked for additional information on the customer's computer. To let customers know that you do not violate certain standards of privacy, you can subscribe to one of the privacy codes that has been promulgated for the Internet. These allow you to put a symbol on your site guaranteeing to your customers that you follow the code.

The websites of two of the organizations that offer this service, and their fees at the time of this publication, are:

www.privacybot.com	$100
www.bbbonline.com	$200 to $6,000

PROTECTING YOURSELF

The easiest way to protect yourself personally from the various possible types of liability is to set up a corporation or limited liability company to own the website. This is not foolproof protection since, in some cases, you could be sued personally as well, but it is one level of protection.

COPPA

If your website is aimed at children under the age of thirteen, or if it attracts children of that age, then you are covered by the federal *Children Online Privacy Protection Act of 1998* (COPPA). This law requires such websites to:

- give notice on the site of what information is being collected;

- obtain verifiable parental consent to collect the information;

- allow the parent to review the information collected;

- allow the parent to delete the child's information or to refuse to allow the use of the information;

- limit the information collected to only that necessary to participate on the site; and,

- protect the security and confidentiality of the information.

FINANCIAL TRANSACTIONS

In the future, there will be easy ways to exchange money on the Internet. Some companies have already been started that promote their own kinds of electronic money. Whether any of these become universal is yet to be seen.

For now, the easiest way to exchange money on the Internet is through traditional credit cards. Because of concerns that email can be abducted in transit and read by others, most companies use a *secure* site in which customers are guaranteed that their card data is encrypted before being sent.

When setting up your website, you should ask the provider if you can be set up with a secure site for transmitting credit card data. If they cannot provide it, you will need to contract with another software provider. Use a major search engine listed on page 149 to look for companies that provide credit card services to businesses on the web.

As a practical matter, there is very little to worry about when sending credit card data by email. If you do not have a secure site, another option is to allow purchasers to fax or phone in their credit card data. However, keep in mind that this extra step will lose some business unless your products are unique and your buyers are very motivated.

The least effective option is to provide an order form on the site, which can be printed out and mailed in with a check. Again, your customers must be really motivated or they will lose interest after finding out this extra work is involved.

FTC Rules

Because the Internet is an instrument of interstate commerce, it is a legitimate subject for federal regulation. The Federal Trade Commission (FTC) first said that all of its consumer protection rules applied to the Internet, but lately it has been adding specific rules and issuing publications. The following publications are available from the FTC website at **www.ftc.gov/bcp/menu-internet.htm** or by mail from Consumer Response Center, Federal Trade Commission, 600 Pennsylvania, NW, Room H-130, Washington, DC 20580-0001.

- *Advertising and Marketing on the Internet: The Rules of the Road*

- *BBB-Online: Code of Online Business Practices*

- *Electronic Commerce: Selling Internationally. A Guide for Business*

- *How to Comply With The Children's Online Privacy Protection Rule*

- *Internet Auctions: A Guide for Buyer and Sellers*

- *Selling on the Internet: Prompt Delivery Rules*

- *Website Woes: Avoiding Web Service Scams*

Fraud

Because the Internet is somewhat anonymous, it is a tempting place for those with fraudulent schemes to look for victims. As a business consumer, you should exercise caution when dealing with unknown or anonymous parties on the Internet.

Recently, the U.S. Department of Justice, the Federal Bureau of Investigation (FBI) and the National White Collar Crime Center launched the Internet Fraud Complaint Center (IFCC). If you suspect that you are the victim of fraud online, whether as a consumer or a business, you can report incidents to the IFCC on their website, **www.ifccfbi.gov**. The IFCC is currently staffed by FBI agents and representatives of the National White Collar Crime Center and will work with state and local law enforcement officials to prevent, investigate, and prosecute high-tech and economic crime online.

BOOKKEEPING AND ACCOUNTING 16

It is beyond the scope of this book to explain all the intricacies of setting up a business' bookkeeping and accounting systems. But the important thing is to realize that if you do not set up an understandable bookkeeping system, your business will undoubtedly fail.

Without accurate records of where your income is coming from and where it is going, you will be unable to increase your profits, lower your expenses, obtain needed financing, or make the right decisions in all areas of your business. The time to decide how you will handle your bookkeeping is when you open your business, not a year later when it is tax time.

INITIAL BOOKKEEPING

If you do not understand business taxation, you should pick up a good book on the subject, as well as the IRS tax guide for your type of business (proprietorship, partnership, or corporation).

The IRS tax book for small businesses is Publication 334, *Tax Guide for Small Businesses*. There are also instruction booklets for each type of business form: Schedule C for proprietorships, Form 1120 or 1120S for C corporations and S corporations, and 1165 for partnerships and businesses which are taxed like partnerships (LLCs, LLPs).

Keep in mind that the IRS does not give you the best advice for saving on taxes and does not give you the other side of contested issues. You need a private tax guide or advisor for that.

The most important thing to do is to set up your bookkeeping so that you can easily fill out your monthly, quarterly, and annual tax returns. The best way to do this is to get copies of the returns, note the categories that you will need to supply, and set up your bookkeeping system to arrive at those totals. For example, for a sole proprietorship you will use "Schedule C" to report business income and expenses to the IRS at the end of the year. Use the categories on that form to sort your expenses. To make your job especially easy, every time you pay a bill, put the category number on the check.

ACCOUNTANTS

Your new business will most likely not be able to afford hiring an accountant right off to handle your books. That is good. Doing your own bookkeeping and tax preparation will force you to learn about business accounting and taxation. The worst way to run a business is to know nothing about the tax laws and turn everything over to an accountant at the end of the year to find out what is due.

You should know the basics of tax law before making basic decisions such as whether to buy or rent equipment or premises. You should understand accounting so you can time your financial affairs appropriately. [If you were a boxer who only needed to win fights, you could turn everything over to an accountant.] If your business needs to buy supplies, inventory, or equipment and provides goods or services throughout the year, you need to at least have a basic understanding of the system within which you are working.

Once you can afford an accountant, you should weigh the cost against your time and the risk that you will make an error. Even if you think you know enough to do your own corporate tax return, you should still take it to an accountant one year to see if you have been missing any deductions. You might decide that the money saved is worth the cost of the accountant's services.

COMPUTER PROGRAMS

Today, every business should keep its books by computer. There are inexpensive programs such as Quicken which can instantly provide you with reports of your income and expenses and the right figures to plug into your tax returns.

Most programs even offer a tax program each year which will take all of your information and print it out on the current year's tax forms.

TAX TIPS

Using these tax tips for small businesses can help you save money:

- Usually when you buy equipment for a business, you must amortize the cost over several years. That is, you do not deduct it all when you buy it, you take, say, twenty-five percent of the cost off your taxes each year for four years. (The time is determined by the theoretical usefulness of the item.) However, small businesses are allowed to write off the entire cost of a limited amount of items under Internal Revenue Code, Section 179. If you have income to shelter, use it.

- Owners of S corporations do not have to pay Social Security or Medicare taxes on the part of their profits that is not considered salary. As long as you pay yourself a reasonable salary, other money you take out is not subject to these taxes.

- You should not neglect to deposit withholding taxes for your own salary or profits. Besides being a large sum to come up with at once in April, there are penalties which must be paid for failure to do so.

- Do not fail to keep track of and remit your employees' withholding. You will be personally liable for them even if you are a corporation.

- If you keep track of the use of your car for business you can deduct 31.5¢ per mile (this may go up or down each year). You may be able to depreciate your car if you use it for business for a considerable amount of time.

- If your business is a corporation and you designate the stock as "section 1244 stock" and the business fails, you are able to get a much better deduction for the loss.

- By setting up a retirement plan, you can exempt up to twenty percent of your salary from income tax. (See Chapter 10.) Do not use money you might need later. There are penalties for taking it out of the retirement plan.

- When you buy things which will be resold or made into products which will be resold, you do not have to pay sales taxes on those purchases. (See Chapter 17.)

PAYING FEDERAL TAXES 17

FEDERAL INCOME TAX

How you pay your taxes will depend upon the type of business entity you start. The manner in which each type of business pays taxes is as follows:

PROPRIETORSHIP   A proprietor reports profits and expenses on a Schedule C, attaches it to the usual **IRS FORM 1040** and pays tax on all of the net income of the business. **IRS FORM ES-1040** must be filed each quarter along with payment of one-quarter of the amount of income tax and social security taxes estimated to be due for the year.

PARTNERSHIP   The partnership files a return showing the income and expenses but pays no tax. Each partner is given a form showing his or her share of the profits or losses and reports these on Schedule E, which is attached to **IRS FORM 1040**. Each quarter, **IRS FORM ES-1040** must be filed by each partner along with payment of one-quarter of the amount of income tax and Social Security taxes estimated to be due for the year.

C CORPORATION   A regular corporation is a separate taxpayer and pays tax on its profits after deducting all expenses, including officers' salaries. If dividends are distributed, they are paid out of after-tax dollars, and the shareholders pay tax a second time on the dividends they receive. If a corporation needs to accumulate money for investment, it may be able to do so at lower tax rates than the shareholders. But if all profits will be distributed to shareholders, the double-taxation may be excessive unless all income is paid as salaries. C corporations file **IRS FORM 1120**.

S CORPORATION

A small corporation has the option of being taxed like a partnership. If **IRS FORM 2553** is filed by the corporation and accepted by the Internal Revenue Service, the S corporation will only file an informational return listing profits and expenses. Each shareholder will be taxed on a proportional share of the profits (or be able to deduct a proportional share of the losses). Unless a corporation will make a large profit that will not be distributed, S-status is usually best in the beginning. An S corporation files **IRS FORM 1120S** and distributes **IRS FORM K-1** to each shareholder. If any money is taken out by a shareholder that is not listed as wages subject to withholding, then the shareholder will usually have to file **IRS FORM ES-1040** each quarter along with payment of the estimated withholding on the withdrawals.

LIMITED LIABILITY
COMPANIES AND
PARTNERSHIPS

Limited liability companies and limited liability partnerships are allowed by the IRS to elect to be taxed either as a partnership or a corporation. To make this election, you file **IRS FORM 8832**, Entity Classification Election, with the IRS. However, you need not file **IRS FORM 8832** if you wish to be treated under the "default rules." These rules provide, among other things, that a "domestic eligible entity" will be treated as a partnership if it has two or more members.

TAX WORKSHOPS
AND BOOKLETS

The IRS conducts workshops to inform businesses about the tax laws. (Do not expect in-depth study of the loopholes.) For information about any of these programs, contact the Taxpayer Education Coordinator at:

617-565-4325 in Boston

800-829-1040 elsewhere

Or, write to: JFK Federal Building
Stop 40726
15 New Sudbury St.
Boston, MA 02203-9112

FEDERAL WITHHOLDING, SOCIAL SECURITY, AND MEDICARE TAXES

If you need basic information on business tax returns, the IRS publishes a rather large booklet that answers most questions and is available free of charge. Call or write them and ask for Publication No. 334. If you have any questions, look up their toll-free number in the phone book under United States Government/Internal Revenue Service. If you want more creative answers and tax saving information, you should find a good local accountant. But to get started, you will need the following:

EMPLOYER IDENTIFICATION NUMBER

If you are a sole proprietor with no employees, you can use your social security number for your business. If you are a corporation, a partnership, or a proprietorship with employees, you must obtain an "Employer Identification Number." This is done by filing FORM SS-4, the APPLICATION FOR EMPLOYER IDENTIFICATION NUMBER. It usually takes a week or two to receive. You will need this number to open bank accounts for the business, so you should file this form a soon as you decide to go into business. A sample filled-in form and instructions are at the end of this chapter.

EMPLOYEE'S WITHHOLDING ALLOWANCE CERTIFICATE

You must have each employee fill out an EMPLOYEES WITHHOLDING ALLOWANCE CERTIFICATE, a W-4 FORM to calculate the amount of federal taxes to be deducted and to obtain their social security numbers. (The number of allowances on this form is used with IRS Circular E, Publication 15, to figure out the exact deductions.) A sample filled-in form is at the end of this chapter.

FEDERAL TAX DEPOSIT COUPONS

After taking withholdings from employees' wages, you must deposit them at a bank which is authorized to accept such funds. If at the end of any month you have over $1,000 in withheld taxes (including your contribution to FICA) you must make a deposit prior to the 15th of the following month. If on the 3rd, 7th, 11th, 15th, 19th, 22nd, or 25th of any month you have over $3,000 in withheld taxes, you must make a deposit within three banking days. The deposit is made using the

165

coupons in the **IRS FORM 8109** booklet. A sample **IRS FORM 8109-B** coupon, which you will use to order your booklet, is shown in Appendix A.

Businesses that make $50,000 or more a year in federal tax deposits are required to use electronic filing.

ESTIMATED TAX PAYMENT VOUCHER

Sole proprietors and partners usually take draws from their businesses without the formality of withholding. However, they are still required to make deposits of income and FICA taxes each quarter. If more than $500 is due in April on a person's 1040 form, then not enough money was withheld each quarter and a penalty is assessed unless the person falls into an exception. The quarterly withholding is submitted on **IRS FORM 1040-ES** on April 15th, June 15th, September 15th, and January 15th each year. If these days fall on a weekend then the due date is the following Monday. The worksheet with **IRS FORM 1040-ES** can be used to determine the amount to pay.

NOTE: *One of the exceptions to the rule is that if you withhold the same amount as last year's tax bill, then you do not have to pay a penalty. This is usually a lot easier than filling out the IRS Form 1040-ES worksheet.*

EMPLOYER'S QUARTERLY TAX RETURN

Each quarter you must file **IRS FORM 941** reporting your federal withholding and FICA taxes. If you owe more than $1,000 at the end of a quarter, you are required to make a deposit at the end of any month that you have $1,000 in withholding. The deposits are made to the Federal Reserve Bank or an authorized financial institution on Form 501. Most banks are authorized to accept deposits. If you owe more than $3,000 for any month, you must make a deposit at any point in the month in which you owe $3,000. After you file **IRS FORM SS-4**, the 941 forms will be sent to you automatically if you checked the box saying that you expect to have employees.

WAGE AND TAX STATEMENT

At the end of each year, you are required to issue an **IRS FORM W-2** to each employee. This form shows the amount of wages paid to the employee during the year as well as the amounts withheld for taxes, Social Security, Medicare, and other purposes. A sample W-2 is in Appendix A.

If you pay at least $600 to a person other than an employee (such as independent contractors), you are required to file an **IRS FORM 1099** for that person. Along with the 1099s, you must file an **IRS FORM 1096**, which is a summary sheet.

Many people are not aware of this law and fail to file these forms, but they are required for such things as services, royalties, rents, awards, and prizes which you pay to individuals (but not corporations). The rules for this are quite complicated so you should either obtain "Package 1099" from the IRS or consult your accountant. Sample forms 1099 and 1096 are in Appendix A.

EARNED INCOME CREDIT

Persons who are not liable to pay income tax may have the right to a check from the government because of the "Earned Income Credit." You are required to notify your employees of this. You can satisfy this requirement with one of the following:

- a **W-2 FORM** with the notice on the back;

- a substitute for the **W-2 FORM** with the notice on it;

- a copy of Notice 797;

- a written statement with the wording from Notice 797; or,

A Notice 797 can be obtained by calling 800-829-3676.

FEDERAL EXCISE TAXES

Excise taxes are taxes on certain activities or items. Most federal excise taxes have been eliminated since World War II, but a few still remain.

Some of the things which are subject to federal excise taxes are tobacco and alcohol, gasoline, tires and inner tubes, some trucks and trailers, firearms, ammunition, bows, arrows, fishing equipment, the use of highway vehicles of over 55,000 pounds, aircraft, wagering, telephone and teletype services, coal, hazardous wastes, and vaccines. If you are involved with any of these, you should obtain from the IRS publication No. 510, *Information on Excise Taxes*.

UNEMPLOYMENT COMPENSATION TAXES

You must pay federal unemployment taxes if you paid wages of $1,500 in any quarter, or if you had at least one employee for twenty calendar weeks. The federal tax amount is 0.8% of the first $7,000 of wages paid each employee. If more than $100 is due by the end of any quarter (if you paid $12,500 in wages for the quarter), then IRS Form 508 must be filed with an authorized financial institution or the Federal Reserve Bank in your area. You will receive IRS Form 508 when you obtain your employer identification number.

At the end of each year, you must file IRS Form 940 or IRS Form 940EZ. This is your annual report of federal unemployment taxes. You will receive an original form from the IRS.

Paying Massachusetts Taxes 18

Sales and Use Tax

If you will be selling or renting goods or services at retail, you must collect Massachusetts Sales and Use Tax. The sales and use tax rate is five percent. Certain items are exempt from sales tax, such as clothing items under $175 and food not bought for immediate consumption. Some services, such as doctors' and lawyers' services and newspaper advertising, are not taxed, but most others are.

The sales tax also applies to meals (it is also called the "Meals Tax"). "Meals" for this purpose is defined as any food or beverage that has been prepared for immediate consumption, including take-out. The meals tax return is similar to the sales tax return. Returns are due monthly.

First, you must obtain a tax number by filling out **Form TA-1** and paying a small fee. A sample filled-in copy of a TA-1 form may be found in Appendix A, and a blank form is contained in Appendix B. For more details about the tax, you should obtain the booklet that comes with **Form TA-1**. You can obtain the form by calling 800-392-6089.

If your sales and use tax liability (excluding meals tax) is reasonably expected to be over $1,200 for the year, you must file monthly returns and pay the taxes due for each month by the twentieth day of the next month. If your liability is under $100, you can file and pay annually; and if between $100 and $1,200, you can file and pay quarterly.

Once you file your FORM TA-1, you will have to start filing returns whether you have any sales or not. A sample monthly sales tax return is provided in Appendix A and a blank form is contained in Appendix B.

One reason to get a tax number early is to exempt your purchases from tax. When you buy a product which you will resell, or use as part of a product which you will sell, you are exempt from paying tax on it. You need to submit a "Resale Certificate" to the seller to get the exemption. This form must contain your sales and use tax registration number.

If you will only be selling items wholesale or out of state, you might think that you do not need a tax number or to submit returns, but you will need to be registered to obtain the tax number to exempt your purchases.

If you have any sales before you get your monthly tax return forms, you should calculate the tax anyway and submit it. Otherwise, you will be charged a penalty regardless of whether or not it was your fault that you did not have the forms.

After you obtain your tax number, you will be required to collect sales tax on all purchases.

If you sell to someone who claims to be exempt from sales and use taxes, (for example, if they plan to resell merchandise they have purchased from you) then they must present to you the previously mentioned Resale Certificate.

INCOME TAX
WITHHOLDING

All employers are required to withhold a portion of their employee's wages for state income tax purposes. If the withheld amount is less than $100 annually, the return is due annually; is between $101 and $1200 annually, the return is due quarterly; if between $1201 and $25,000 annually, the return is due monthly; if over $25,000 annually, the return periods vary but can be required weekly. A sample monthly withholding tax return is shown on page 224, and a blank form is contained in Appendix B.

ROOM
OCCUPANCY TAX

Individuals operating hotels, motels, lodging houses or private clubs offering sleeping accommodations must pay room occupancy tax of 5.7 percent on rooms rented for $15 or more per day, to persons occupying the rooms for 90 consecutive days or less. Returns are due monthly.

CIGARETTE AND
TOBACCO TAX

The state also imposes taxes on the sale of cigarettes, smoking tobacco, and cigars. Returns are due monthly.

CORPORATE EXCISE (INCOME) TAX

Massachusetts taxes corporations based on their Massachusetts income, and their tangible and intangible property. The minimum tax (even for S corporations) is $456 per year. Estimated tax payments must be made during the year if your liability will be over $1,000 for the year.

The corporate income tax rate is 9.5% on income attributable to Massachusetts. Contact the Massachusetts Department of Revenue for more information.

UNEMPLOYMENT COMPENSATION TAXES

You are not liable to pay unemployment compensation taxes until you have had an employee work a part of a day in any thirteen calendar weeks, or paid $1,500 in wages in a quarter. But once you reach that point, you are liable for all back taxes. The rate varies according to your employment record. The tax is paid on the first $10,800 of wages of each employee.

If you anticipate having an employee for thirteen weeks or when you have had an employee work for thirteen weeks, you should file an EMPLOYER'S STATUS REPORT, FORM 1110-A. A sample filled-in FORM 1110-A may be found on page 232, and a blank form is included in Appendix B. You will be sent quarterly returns to complete.

The Department of Revenue's Website, at **www.dor.state.ma.us**, has a wealth of information, instructions and forms to assist the business owner in complying with the state's tax requirements. Many of the returns can be filed electronically. See a list of online state tax forms at **www.dor.state.ma.us/forms/formlist.htm**. Also, a very helpful state tax guide for businesses can be found at:

www.dor.state.ma.us/bsbc/taxes/taxguide/toc.htm.

Out-of-State Taxes 19

State Sales Taxes

In 1992, the United States Supreme Court safeguarded the rights of small businesses by ruling that state tax authorities cannot force them to collect sales taxes on interstate mail orders (*Quill Corporation v. North Dakota*).

Unfortunately, the court left open the possibility that Congress could allow interstate taxation of mail order sales, and several bills have since been introduced which would do so. One, introduced by Arkansas senator Dale Bumpers, was given the Orwellian "newspeak" title, *The Consumer and Main Street Protection Act*.

At present, companies are only required to collect sales taxes for states in which they *do business*. Exactly what business is enough to trigger taxation is a legal question and some states try to define it as broadly as possible.

If you have an office in a state, you are doing business there and any goods shipped to consumers in that state are subject to sales taxes. If you have a full time employee working in the state most of the year, many states will consider you doing business there. In some states, attending a two-day trade show is enough business to trigger taxation for the entire year for every order shipped to the state. One loophole that often works is to be represented at shows by persons who are not your employees.

Because the laws are different in each state, you will have to do some research on a state-by-state basis to find out how much business you can do in a state without being subject to their taxation. You can request a state's rules from its department of revenue, but keep in mind that what a department of revenue wants the law to be is not always what the courts will rule that it is.

BUSINESS TAXES

Being subject to a state's income or other business taxes is even worse than being bound to a state's sales taxes. For example, California charges every company doing business in the state a minimum $800 a year fee and charges income tax on a portion of the company's worldwide income. Doing a small amount of business in the state is clearly not worth getting mired in California taxation.

For this reason, some trade shows have been moved from the state and this has resulted in a review of the tax policies and some "safe-harbor" guidelines to advise companies on what they can do without becoming subject to taxation.

Write to the department of revenue of any state with which you have business contacts to see what might trigger your taxation.

INTERNET TAXES

State revenue departments are drooling at the prospect of taxing commerce on the Internet. Theories have already been proposed that websites available to state residents mean a company is doing business in a state.

Fortunately, Congress has passed a moratorium on taxation of the Internet. This will be extended, hopefully, and will give us a new tax-free world, but do not count on it. A government has never let a new source of revenue go untapped. It would take a tremendous outcry to keep the Internet tax-free. Perhaps the Internet can be used as a new "enterprise zone" to encourage business growth. Keep an eye out for any news stories on proposals to tax the Internet and petition your representatives against them.

If laws are passed to tax the Internet, there is a new opportunity for some businesses. For many types of businesses, especially companies which can provide their goods or services over the Internet, it would be possible to set up the business on a tax-free Caribbean island. With no state presence, no taxes would be due to any state.

CANADIAN TAXES

Apparently oblivious to the logic of the U.S. Supreme Court, the Canadian government expects American companies, which sell goods by mail order to Canadians, to collect taxes for them and file returns with Revenue Canada, their tax department.

Those that receive an occasional unsolicited order are not expected to register, and Canadian customers who order things from the U.S. pay the tax plus a $5 fee upon receipt of the goods. Nonetheless, companies that solicit Canadian orders are expected to be registered if their worldwide income is $30,000 or more per year. In some cases, a company may be required to post a bond and to pay for the cost of Canadian auditors visiting its premises and auditing its books! You may notice that some companies decline to accept orders from Canada for these reasons.

THE END...AND THE BEGINNING

If you have read through this whole book, you know more about the rules and laws for operating a Massachusetts business than most people in business today. However, after learning about all the governmental regulations, you may become discouraged. You are probably wondering how you can keep track of all the laws and how you will have any time left to make money after complying with the laws. It is not that bad. People are starting businesses every day and they are making money, lots of money. American business owners are lucky—some countries have marginal tax rates as high as 105%!

The regulations that exist right now are enough to strangle some businesses. Consider the Armour meat-packing plant. The Federal Meat Inspection Service required that an opening be made in a conveyor to allow inspection or they would shut down the plant. OSHA told them that if they made that opening they would be shut down for safety reasons. Government regulations made it impossible for that plant to be in business!

In a pure democracy, fifty-one percent of the voters can decide that all left-handed people must wear green shirts and that everyone must go to church three days a week. It is the Bill of Rights in our constitution that protects us from the tyrannical whims of the majority.

In America today, there are no laws regarding left-handed people or going to church but there are laws controlling minute aspects of our personal and business lives. Does a majority have the right to decide what hours you can work, what you can sell or where you can sell it? You must decide for yourself and act accordingly.

One way to avoid problems with the government is to keep a low profile and avoid open confrontation. For a lawyer, it can be fun going to appeals court over an unfair parking ticket or making a federal case out of a $25 fine. But for most people the expenses of a fight with the government are unbearable. If you start a mass protest against the IRS or OSHA they will have to make an example of you so that no one else gets any ideas.

The important thing is that you know the laws and the penalties for violations before making your decision. Knowing the laws will also allow you to use the loopholes in the laws to avoid violations.

GLOSSARY

A

authorized shares. When a corporation is formed, it is divided into parts called shares. A certain number of shares are authorized by filing organizational documents with the state. The number authorized may be changed later by shareholder vote and amendment to the organizational documents. The corporation may not at any time issue a number of shares greater than the number authorized. The shares issued, also called "outstanding" or "issued and outstanding," at any point in time comprise the entire ownership of the company. In theory, there could be only one share authorized and issued, owned by one person, which would comprise 100% of the ownership of the company.

More often, the corporation is formed with multiple shares authorized, which can range from a small number (often 200 shares, especially in Massachusetts) to a large number (50,000,000 shares or more). The right number of shares to choose depends on several factors—for example, the number of current owners and potential owners, and the fees charged by each state for authorizing shares. Not all authorized shares need be issued—some, or most, can be reserved for future use (for example, an IPO).

B

business certificate. Also called "fictitious name certificate." Filing that must be made with town or city clerk by persons and entities doing business under a name other than their true legal name, also called a "trade name" or "fictitious name."

buy-sell agreement. An agreement among shareholders governing the sale or other transfer of shares, and usually including what happens if a shareholder working for the corporation leaves the job or is fired, or dies or becomes disabled. Buy-Sell Agreements can also include voting agreements regarding the voting of shares, and other corporate governance provisions.

State law may limit the enforceability of certain provisions. One common example is a provision that the company will secure life insurance for each owner, with the company listed as the beneficiary. If one such owner should die, the company would use the proceeds of the life insurance to buy the deceased owner's share from his or her spouse, or others who may inherit the share of the company. This serves to provide a cash death benefit to the deceased owner's loved ones, and gives those loved ones a way to get cash out of the company upon the owner's demise. It also protects the surviving business owner(s) from having unwanted, or worse, co-owners.

C

C corporation. One of the types of entities under which you may do business and achieve the protections of limited liability – that is, unless the "corporate veil" is "pierced," only the assets of the entity, not those of its owners, can be used to satisfy liabilities and obligations incurred by that business. C corporations may have unlimited numbers of shareholders. Publicly traded companies are C corporations.

copyright. The legal right granted to an author, composer, playwright, publisher, or distributor to exclusive publication, production, sale, or distribution of a literary, musical, dramatic, or artistic work. This allows the copyright's owner to (a) prevent a copier from using the copy or copies, and (b) compensatory damages under certain conditions.

corporation. A body that is granted a charter recognizing it as a separate legal entity having its own rights, privileges, and liabilities distinct from those of its members. Corporations are entities created by the state in which they are formed. There are no "federal" corporations; each one is registered and created by a state. Once corporations are established, they may be registered to do business in other states. Doing business through a corporation is one way to protect the owners' personal assets.

D

Department of Revenue (Mass.). The state agency, also called the "DOR" responsible for collecting state taxes, enforcing state tax laws, and educating the public about state tax requirements.

domain name. A series of letters used to name organizations, computers and addresses on the Internet. Every computer on the Internet has an "address" which is a series of numbers much like a telephone number. (In technical jargon that address is called the "IP" address. IP stands for Internet Protocol.) The Domain Name System allows the use of more familiar names to reference those computers. There cannot be duplicate names. Each name is linked by the registration system to the unique string of numbers used to identify the computers. Once a name is taken, someone else cannot use it unless the first party relinquishes the name. Domain names must be registered, which can be done through a number of registration services (search for 'domain name registration' in any search engine and several companies will appear).

E

employee.   A worker who is subject to the supervision and control of management with respect to the manner and means of work done.

F

fictitious name.   *See business certificate.*

G

general partnership.   *See partnership.*

I

independent contractor.   A person who works on his own, rather than as an employee. If management has the right to supervise and control the manner and means of work done by an individual, that individual is normally called an "employee." If a worker controls his or her own work methods, works for more than one entity, sets his or her own hours, and provides his or her own equipment, the person will usually be deemed an "independent contractor." Taxes are collected and paid differently with respect to employees vs. independent contractors.

initial public offering (IPO).   The first time a corporation offers its stock to the public, or "goes public." This is different from a "private placement," where stock or other securities may be offered to a limited number of individuals, or individuals who meet certain criteria.

L

limited. One of the words that many states allow in a corporation's name as an indication that the company is of limited liability status. All states require corporations to use a word such as corporation, incorporated, or limited to indicate to the public that the entity is a limited liability entity.

limited liability company (LLC). A legal entity with characteristics of both a corporation and a partnership. The tax treatment of an LLC is similar to that of a partnership—that is, the income is not taxed at the entity level, but at the equity owner level. But the LLC also has the benefit of limited liability, meaning that the owners are not personally liable for the business's debts and obligations. Its limited liability protection is similar to that of a corporation.

limited liability entity. An entity whose equity owners are not personally liable for the entity's debts and obligations, such as a corporation, LLC, or LLP.

limited liability partnership. An entity similar to a partnership, but where the personal liability of each partner is limited. Devised to allow partnerships of lawyers and other professionals limit their personal liability without losing the partnership structure. Does not protect against malpractice or professional responsibility.

limited partnership. A legal entity that is somewhat similar to a partnership. In a limited partnership, there are one or more general partner(s), who do not enjoy limited liability status, and one or more limited partners, who do. The limited partners cannot participate in the running of the entity's business, or their limited liability status will be jeopardized.

M

Massachusetts Commission Against Discrimination (MCAD). State agency responsible for enforcing the state's anti-discrimination laws.

N

noncompete. A contract restricting the right of a person to compete against another, usually a former employer. Also used by buyers of businesses to keep the business seller from competing.

nonprofit corporation. A corporation formed under a separate set of laws than those for business corporations, usually used by churches, condominium associations, and other groups not seeking profits.

P

partnership. An arrangement between two or more persons who agree to pool talent and money and share profits or losses, for the purpose of undertaking some sort of business. Also called "general partnership."

patent. A property right granted by the government to an inventor to exclude others from making, using, offering for sale, or selling the invention in a territory or importing the invention into the territory for a limited time in exchange for public disclosure of the invention when the patent is granted.

piercing the corporate veil. Holding the equity owners of a corporation or limited liability company personally liable for the company's debts and liabilities. This is a legal remedy that can be used to obtain assets of a company's shareholders or equity owners to satisfy a judgment against the company. A court will only allow the "piercing of the veil" in limited circumstances. Some of the factors which may lead a court to "pierce the veil" are commingling of personal and company assets; failure to observe company formalities; failing to hold oneself out to the public as a limited liability entity; undercapitalization; use of company assets for personal purposes; and failure to make legally required filings.

private placement. An offer and sale of securities by an entity to a limited number or category of persons.

professional corporation. A corporation owned and run by certain professionals such as accountants, lawyers and doctors. Most states allow certain professionals to incorporate only as a professional corporation. Although the corporation does have limited liability status, it does not protect the professionals from malpractice liability nor does it alter professional responsibility or privilege.

proprietorship. A business owned and run by one person, and not incorporated or otherwise enjoying limited liability protection.

S

S corporation. A corporation that has made an official election under federal law to be treated similarly to a partnership for purposes of tax law. The tax attributes of the corporation flow through to its equity owners and are taxed only at the owner level. This is called "flow-through" taxation. In certain states, a state-level filing is also required for the corporation to receive the same tax treatment at the state level.

service mark. Same thing as a trademark, except that it identifies and distinguishes the source of a service rather than a product.

shareholders' agreement. *See buy-sell agreement.*

T

territory. Area covered by a contract, covenant, license, right, or the like, such as a non-compete or patent.

trade name. *See business certificate.*

trademark.   Any word, name, symbol, or device, or any combination, used, or intended to be used, in commerce to identify and distinguish the goods of one manufacturer or seller from goods manufactured or sold by others, and to indicate the source of the goods. A brand name.

U

Uniform Commercial Code (UCC).   A set of laws adopted by almost every state in the U.S. (with variations), governing sales of goods, secured transactions, and other commercial matters.

usury.   Interest charged at a rate which is excessive or higher than that allowed by law.

For Further Reference

The following books will provide valuable information to those who are starting new businesses. Some are out of print, but they are classics that are worth tracking down.

For inspiration to give you the drive to succeed:

Hill, Napoleon, *Think and Grow Rich*. New York: Fawcett Books, 1990, 233 pages.

Karbo, Joe, *The Lazy Man's Way to Riches*. Sunset Beach: F P Publishing, 1974, 156 pages.

Schwartz, David J., *The Magic of Thinking Big*. Fireside, 1987, 234 pages.

For hints on what it takes to be successful:

Carnegie, Dale, *How to Win Friends and Influence People*. New York: Pocket Books, 1994, 276 pages.

Ringer, Robert J., *Looking Out for #1*. New York: Fawcett Books, 1993.

Ringer, Robert J., *Million Dollar Habits*. New York: Fawcett Books, 1991.

Ringer, Robert J., *Winning Through Intimidation*. New York: Fawcett Books, 1993.

For advice on bookkeeping and organization:

Kamoroff, Bernard, *Small Time Operator (25th Edition)*. Bell Springs Publishing, 2000, 200 pages.

For a very practical guide to investing:

Tobias, Andrew, *The Only Investment Guide You'll Ever Need*. Harvest Books, 1999, 239 pages.

For advice on how to avoid problems with government agencies:

Browne, Harry, *How I Found Freedom in an Unfree World*. Great Falls: Liam Works, 1998, 387 pages.

The following are other books published by **Sphinx Publishing** that may be helpful to your business:

Eckert, W. Kelsea; Arthur Sartorius , III; and Mark Warda, *How to Form Your Own Corporation (3rd Edition)*. 2001.

Haman, Edward A., *How to Form Your Own Partnership (2nd Edition)*. 2002.

Barreca, Hugo, and O'Neill, Julia K., *The Entrepreneur's Internet Handbook*. 2002.

Ray, James C., *The Most Valuable Business Legal Forms You'll Ever Need (3rd Edition)*. 2001.

Ray, James C., *The Complete Book of Corporate Forms*. 2001.

Warda, Mark, *How to Form a Delaware Corporation from Any State*. 2000.

Warda, Mark, *Incorporate in Nevada from Any State*. 2001.

Warda, Mark, *How to Form a Limited Liability Company*. 1999.

Warda, Mark, *How to Register Your Own Copyright (4th Edition)*. 2002.

Warda, Mark, *How to Register Your Own Trademark (3rd Edition)*. 2000.

The following are books published by **Sourcebooks, Inc.** that may be helpful to your business:

Fleury, Robert E., *The Small Business Survival Guide.*. 1995.

Gutman, Jean E., *Accounting Made Easy*. 1998.

Milling, Bryan E., *How to Get a Small Business Loan (2nd Edition)*. 1998.

The following websites provide information that may be useful to you in starting your business:

Internal Revenue Service: www.irs.gov

Small Business Administration: www.sba.gov

Social Security Administration: www.ssa.gov

United States Patent and Trademark Office: www..uspto.gov

United States Copyright Office: http://lcweb.loc.gov/copyright

United States Code (statutes): http://uscode.house.gov/usc.htm

Code of Federal Regulations: www.access.gpo.gov/nara/cfr/cfr-table-search.html

The Commonwealth of Massachusetts: www.mass.gov

Massachusetts Corporations Division: www.state.ma.us/sec/cor/coridx.htm

General Laws of Massachusetts: www.state.ma.us/legis/laws/mgl/index.htm

Massachusetts Department of Revenue: www.dor.state.ma.us

Massachusetts State Tax Guide for Businesses:

www.dor.state.ma.us/bsbc/taxes/taxguide/toc.htm

APPENDIX A
SAMPLE FILLED-IN FORMS

The following forms may be photocopied or removed from this book and used immediately. Some of the tax forms explained in this book are not included here because you should use original returns provided by the IRS (940, 941) or the Massachusetts Department of Revenue (quarterly unemployment compensation form). Be sure to check with the proper authorities in case there are any additional requirements.

TABLE OF FORMS

The Commonwealth of Massachusetts

William Francis Galvin
Secretary of the Commonwealth
One Ashburton Place, Boston, Massachusetts 02108-1512

APPLICATION FOR REGISTRATION OF A TRADEMARK
(General Laws, Chapter 110B, Section 2)

1. Name of applicant: Mickey the Marble Bengal, Inc.

2. (a) Principal business address: 2 Wildlife Dr., Marlborough, MA 12345

   (b) *Business address in Massachusetts, if any:

3. State whether applicant is an individual, partnership, corporation, union or association: Corporation

4. If a corporation, the state of incorporation is: Massachusetts

5. Describe mark: Mickey's Marbles

6. Describe the specific goods in connection with which the mark is used: Marbles

7. Class No.: 28

8. The mark is used by displaying it:

   ☐ directly to the goods
   ☐ directly to the containers for the goods
   ☐ by displaying it in physical association with the goods in the sale or distribution thereof
   ☐ in other fashions (explain):

   ☒ to tags or labels affixed to the containers for the goods
   ☐ to tags or labels affixed directly to the goods

9. Date of first use of mark by applicant or predecessor. If first use of mark was in Massachusetts, use the same date in both (a) and (b).

   (a) Anywhere: 3/11/03

   (b) In Massachusetts: 3/11/03

10. If either of the above first uses was by a predecessor of the applicant, state which use or uses were by a predecessor and identify that predecessor:

Name of applicant: Mickey the Marble Bengal, Inc.

State of: Mass.

County of: Middlesex

Signature of applicant: *Mickey Fleming, Pres.*

Title: President

Note: This document must be notarized – see reverse side.
Fill in only if principal business address is not in Massachusetts

_____ , being duly sworn, deposes and says that he is the _____

of the above named applicant, that the statements contained in the foregoing statement are true and that he verily believes that said applicant is the owner of the mark sought to be registered and that no other person has the right in the Commonwealth of Massachusetts to use such mark either in the identical form thereof, or in such near resemblance thereto, as to be likely, when applied to the goods or services of such person, to cause confusion or to cause mistake or to deceive.

SUBSCRIBED and sworn to before me this _____ day of _____ , 20 _____.

Notary Public: _____   My commission expires: _____

Please print the name and address in the space provided below of the person to whom you wish this application to be sent.

CERTIFICATE OF REGISTRATION OF A TRADEMARK

General Laws, Chapter 110B, Section 4

Filed with
William Francis Galvin,
Secretary of the Commonwealth
and Secretary's Certificate of Record issued on:

_____ , 20 _____

William Francis Galvin
Secretary of the Commonwealth
Trademark Section
One Ashburton Place, Rm. 1712
Boston, MA 02108

* _____

_____

_____

_____

U.S. Department of Justice
Immigration and Naturalization Service

OMB No. 1115-0136

Employment Eligibility Verification

INSTRUCTIONS
PLEASE READ ALL INSTRUCTIONS CAREFULLY BEFORE COMPLETING THIS FORM.

Anti-Discrimination Notice. It is illegal to discriminate against any individual (other than an alien not authorized to work in the U.S.) in hiring, discharging, or recruiting or referring for a fee because of that individual's national origin or citizenship status. It is illegal to discriminate against work eligible individuals. Employers **CANNOT** specify which document(s) they will accept from an employee. The refusal to hire an individual because of a future expiration date may also constitute illegal discrimination.

Section 1 - Employee.
All employees, citizens and noncitizens, hired after November 6, 1986, must complete Section 1 of this form at the time of hire, which is the actual beginning of employment. **The employer is responsible for ensuring that Section 1 is timely and properly completed.**

Preparer/Translator Certification. The Preparer/Translator Certification must be completed if Section 1 is prepared by a person other than the employee. A preparer/translator may be used only when the employee is unable to complete Section 1 on his/her own. However, the employee must still sign Section 1.

Section 2 - Employer.
For the purpose of completing this form, the term "employer" includes those recruiters and referrers for a fee who are agricultural associations, agricultural employers or farm labor contractors.

Employers must complete Section 2 by examining evidence of identity and employment eligibility within three (3) business days of the date employment begins. If employees are authorized to work, but are unable to present the required document(s) within three business days, they must present a receipt for the application of the document(s) within three business days and the actual document(s) within ninety (90) days. However, if employers hire individuals for a duration of less than three business days, Section 2 must be completed at the time employment begins. **Employers must record: 1)** document title; **2)** issuing authority; **3)** document number, **4)** expiration date, if any; and **5)** the date employment begins. Employers must sign and date the certification. Employees must present original documents. Employers may, but are not required to, photocopy the document(s) presented. These photocopies may only be used for the verification process and must be retained with the I-9. **However, employers are still responsible for completing the I-9.**

Section 3 - Updating and Reverification.
Employers must complete Section 3 when updating and/or reverifying the I-9. Employers must reverify employment eligibility of their employees on or before the expiration date recorded in Section 1. Employers **CANNOT** specify which document(s) they will accept from an employee.

- If an employee's name has changed at the time this form is being updated/ reverified, complete Block A.

- If an employee is rehired within three (3) years of the date this form was originally completed and the employee is still eligible to be employed on the same basis as previously indicated on this form (updating), complete Block B and the signature block.

- If an employee is rehired within three (3) years of the date this form was originally completed and the employee's work authorization has expired **or** if a current employee's work authorization is about to expire (reverification), complete Block B and:
  - examine any document that reflects that the employee is authorized to work in the U.S. (see List A **or** C),
  - record the document title, document number and expiration date (if any) in Block C, and complete the signature block.

Photocopying and Retaining Form I-9. A blank I-9 may be reproduced, provided both sides are copied. The Instructions must be available to all employees completing this form. Employers must retain completed I-9s for three (3) years after the date of hire or one (1) year after the date employment ends, whichever is later.

For more detailed information, you may refer to the INS Handbook for Employers, (Form M-274). You may obtain the handbook at your local INS office.

Privacy Act Notice. The authority for collecting this information is the Immigration Reform and Control Act of 1986, Pub. L. 99-603 (8 USC 1324a).

This information is for employers to verify the eligibility of individuals for employment to preclude the unlawful hiring, or recruiting or referring for a fee, of aliens who are not authorized to work in the United States.

This information will be used by employers as a record of their basis for determining eligibility of an employee to work in the United States. The form will be kept by the employer and made available for inspection by officials of the U.S. Immigration and Naturalization Service, the Department of Labor and the Office of Special Counsel for Immigration Related Unfair Employment Practices.

Submission of the information required in this form is voluntary. However, an individual may not begin employment unless this form is completed, since employers are subject to civil or criminal penalties if they do not comply with the Immigration Reform and Control Act of 1986.

Reporting Burden. We try to create forms and instructions that are accurate, can be easily understood and which impose the least possible burden on you to provide us with information. Often this is difficult because some immigration laws are very complex. Accordingly, the reporting burden for this collection of information is computed as follows: **1)** learning about this form, 5 minutes; **2)** completing the form, 5 minutes; and **3)** assembling and filing (recordkeeping) the form, 5 minutes, for an average of 15 minutes per response. If you have comments regarding the accuracy of this burden estimate, or suggestions for making this form simpler, you can write to the Immigration and Naturalization Service, HQPDI, 425 I Street, N.W., Room 4034, Washington, DC 20536. OMB No. 1115-0136.

EMPLOYERS MUST RETAIN COMPLETED FORM I-9
PLEASE DO NOT MAIL COMPLETED FORM I-9 TO INS

Form I-9 (Rev. 11-21-91)N

Please read instructions carefully before completing this form. The instructions must be available during completion of this form. ANTI-DISCRIMINATION NOTICE: It is illegal to discriminate against work eligible individuals. Employers CANNOT specify which document(s) they will accept from an employee. The refusal to hire an individual because of a future expiration date may also constitute illegal discrimination.

Section 1. Employee Information and Verification. To be completed and signed by employee at the time employment begins.

Print Name: Last	First	Middle Initial	Maiden Name
ANDREWS	DOUGLAS	F.	

Address (Street Name and Number)	Apt. #	Date of Birth (month/day/year)
12 PORTOBELLO RD.		5/8/64

City	State	Zip Code	Social Security #
EDINBURGH MA		55555	555-66-2222

I am aware that federal law provides for imprisonment and/or fines for false statements or use of false documents in connection with the completion of this form.

I attest, under penalty of perjury, that I am (check one of the following):
- [X] A citizen or national of the United States
- [ ] A Lawful Permanent Resident (Alien # A
- [ ] An alien authorized to work until ___/___/___
(Alien # or Admission #)

Employee's Signature *Douglas F. Andrews*	Date (month/day/year) 1/29/03

Preparer and/or Translator Certification. (To be completed and signed if Section 1 is prepared by a person other than the employee.) I attest, under penalty of perjury, that I have assisted in the completion of this form and that to the best of my knowledge the information is true and correct.

Preparer's/Translator's Signature	Print Name

Address (Street Name and Number, City, State, Zip Code)	Date (month/day/year)

Section 2. Employer Review and Verification. To be completed and signed by employer. Examine one document from List A OR examine one document from List B and one from List C, as listed on the reverse of this form, and record the title, number and expiration date, if any, of the document(s)

List A	OR	List B	AND	List C
Document title: PASSPORT		_____		_____
Issuing authority: PASSPORT AGENCY PTB		_____		_____
Document #: 123456789		_____		_____
Expiration Date (if any): 10/5/06		___/___/___		___/___/___
Document #: _____				
Expiration Date (if any): ___/___/___				

CERTIFICATION - I attest, under penalty of perjury, that I have examined the document(s) presented by the above-named employee, that the above-listed document(s) appear to be genuine and to relate to the employee named, that the employee began employment on (month/day/year) 02/03/03 **and that to the best of my knowledge the employee is eligible to work in the United States. (State employment agencies may omit the date the employee began employment.)**

Signature of Employer or Authorized Representative *Darron Krebbs*	Print Name Darron Krebbs	Title owner

Business or Organization Name	Address (Street Name and Number, City, State, Zip Code)	Date (month/day/year)
Krebbs Company	100 Maynard Dr., Edinburgh, MA 55554	2/3/03

Section 3. Updating and Reverification. To be completed and signed by employer.

A. New Name (if applicable)	B. Date of rehire (month/day/year) (if applicable)

C. If employee's previous grant of work authorization has expired, provide the information below for the document that establishes current employment eligibility.

Document Title:_____ Document #: _____ Expiration Date (if any): ___/___/___

I attest, under penalty of perjury, that to the best of my knowledge, this employee is eligible to work in the United States, and if the employee presented document(s), the document(s) I have examined appear to be genuine and to relate to the individual.

Signature of Employer or Authorized Representative	Date (month/day/year)

Form **SS-4**	**Application for Employer Identification Number**	EIN
(Rev. December 2001) Department of the Treasury Internal Revenue Service	(For use by employers, corporations, partnerships, trusts, estates, churches, government agencies, Indian tribal entities, certain individuals, and others.) · See separate instructions for each line. · Keep a copy for your records.	OMB No. 1545-0003

Type or print clearly.

1 Legal name of entity (or individual) for whom the EIN is being requested

Ollie the Hound Dog, Inc.

2 Trade name of business (if different from name on line 1)

n/a

3 Executor, trustee, "care of" name

4a Mailing address (room, apt., suite no. and street, or P.O. box)

1 Always Underfoot Rd.

5a Street address (if different) (Do not enter a P.O. box.)

4b City, state, and ZIP code

Holliston, MA 01746

5b City, state, and ZIP code

6 County and state where principal business is located

Middlesex, MA

7a Name of principal officer, general partner, grantor, owner, or trustor

Ollie D. Goofball

7b SSN, ITIN, or EIN

999-99-9999

8a **Type of entity** (check only one box)

- [X] Sole proprietor (SSN) _____
- [ ] Partnership
- [ ] Corporation (enter form number to be filed) · _____
- [ ] Personal service corp.
- [ ] Church or church-controlled organization
- [ ] Other nonprofit organization (specify) · _____
- [ ] Other (specify) · _____

- [ ] Estate (SSN of decedent) _____
- [ ] Plan administrator (SSN) _____
- [ ] Trust (SSN of grantor) _____
- [ ] National Guard   [ ] State/local government
- [ ] Farmers' cooperative   [ ] Federal government/military
- [ ] REMIC   [ ] Indian tribal governments/enterprises
- Group Exemption Number (GEN) · _____

8b If a corporation, name the state or foreign country (if applicable) where incorporated

State	Foreign country

9 **Reason for applying** (check only one box)

- [X] Started new business (specify type) · _____
  bark sales
- [ ] Hired employees (Check the box and see line 12.)
- [ ] Compliance with IRS withholding regulations
- [ ] Other (specify) ·

- [ ] Banking purpose (specify purpose) · _____
- [ ] Changed type of organization (specify new type) · _____
- [ ] Purchased going business
- [ ] Created a trust (specify type) · _____
- [ ] Created a pension plan (specify type) · _____

10 Date business started or acquired (month, day, year)

10-15-2002

11 Closing month of accounting year

December

12 First date wages or annuities were paid or will be paid (month, day, year). **Note:** *If applicant is a withholding agent, enter date income will first be paid to nonresident alien. (month, day, year)* . . . . · 10-22-2002

13 Highest number of employees expected in the next 12 months. **Note:** *If the applicant does not expect to have any employees during the period, enter "-0-."* . . . . ·

Agricultural	Household	Other

14 Check **one** box that best describes the principal activity of your business.

- [ ] Construction [ ] Rental & leasing [ ] Transportation & warehousing
- [ ] Real estate [ ] Manufacturing [ ] Finance & insurance
- [ ] Health care & social assistance
- [ ] Accommodation & food service
- [ ] Other (specify)
- [X] Wholesale–agent/broker
- [ ] Wholesale–other   [ ] Retail

15 Indicate principal line of merchandise sold; specific construction work done; products produced; or services provided.

bark sales

16a Has the applicant ever applied for an employer identification number for this or any other business? . . . . . [ ] **Yes** [X] **No**
Note: *If "Yes," please complete lines 16b and 16c.*

16b If you checked "Yes" on line 16a, give applicant's legal name and trade name shown on prior application if different from line 1 or 2 above.
Legal name ·   Trade name ·

16c Approximate date when, and city and state where, the application was filed. Enter previous employer identification number if known.

Approximate date when filed (mo., day, year)	City and state where filed	Previous EIN

Third Party Designee	Complete this section **only** if you want to authorize the named individual to receive the entity's EIN and answer questions about the completion of this form.	
	Designee's name	Designee's telephone number (include area code) ( )
	Address and ZIP code	Designee's fax number (include area code) ( )

Under penalties of perjury, I declare that I have examined this application, and to the best of my knowledge and belief, it is true, correct, and complete.

Name and title (type or print clearly) ·   Ollie D. Goofball, owner

Applicant's telephone number (include area code)
(518) 555-0000

Signature · *Ollie D. Goofball*   Date · 10/20/2002

Applicant's fax number (include area code)
(   )

For Privacy Act and Paperwork Reduction Act Notice, see separate instructions.   Cat. No. 16055N   Form **SS-4** (Rev. 12-2001)

rm W-4 (2003)

ose. Complete Form W-4 so that your
loyer can withhold the correct Federal
me tax from your pay. Because your tax sit-
n may change, you may want to refigure
withholding each year.

nption from withholding. If you are
npt, complete only lines 1, 2, 3, 4, and 7 and
the form to validate it. Your exemption for
3 expires February 16, 2004. See **Pub. 505,**
Withholding and Estimated Tax.

: *You cannot claim exemption from with-
ing if: (a) your income exceeds $750 and
des more than $250 of unearned income
, interest and dividends) and (b) another
on can claim you as a dependent on their
return.*

ic instructions. If you are not exempt, com-
e the **Personal Allowances Worksheet**
w. The worksheets on page 2 adjust your
holding allowances based on itemized

deductions, certain credits, adjustments to
income, or two-earner/two-job situations. Complete all worksheets that apply. **However, you
may claim fewer (or zero) allowances.**

Head of household. Generally, you may claim
head of household filing status on your tax
return only if you are unmarried and pay more
than 50% of the costs of keeping up a home for
yourself and your dependent(s) or other qualify-
ing individuals. See line **E** below.

Tax credits. You can take projected tax credits
into account in figuring your allowable number of
withholding allowances. Credits for child or
dependent care expenses and the child tax
credit may be claimed using the **Personal
Allowances Worksheet** below. See **Pub. 919,**
How Do I Adjust My Tax Withholding? for information on converting your other credits into
withholding allowances.

Nonwage income. If you have a large amount of
nonwage income, such as interest or dividends,
consider making estimated tax payments using

Form 1040-ES, Estimated Tax for Individuals.
Otherwise, you may owe additional tax.

Two earners/two jobs. If you have a working
spouse or more than one job, figure the total
number of allowances you are entitled to claim
on all jobs using worksheets from only one Form
W-4. Your withholding usually will be most accurate when all allowances are claimed on the
Form W-4 for the highest paying job and zero
allowances are claimed on the others.

Nonresident alien. If you are a nonresident
alien, see the **Instructions for Form 8233** before
completing this Form W-4.

Check your withholding. After your Form W-4
takes effect, use Pub. 919 to see how the dollar
amount you are having withheld compares to
your projected total tax for 2003. See Pub. 919,
especially if your earnings exceed $125,000
(Single) or $175,000 (Married).

Recent name change? If your name on line 1
differs from that shown on your social security
card, call 1-800-772-1213 for a new social security card.

Personal Allowances Worksheet (Keep for your records.)

Enter "1" for **yourself** if no one else can claim you as a dependent . . . . **A** ____

Enter "1" if:
- You are single and have only one job; or
- You are married, have only one job, and your spouse does not work; or ⟩ . . **B** 1
- Your wages from a second job or your spouse's wages (or the total of both) are $1,000 or less.

Enter "1" for your **spouse.** But, you may choose to enter "-0-" if you are married and have either a working spouse or
more than one job. (Entering "-0-" may help you avoid having too little tax withheld.) . . . . **C** ____

Enter number of **dependents** (other than your spouse or yourself) you will claim on your tax return . . . . . . **D** ____

Enter "1" if you will file as **head of household** on your tax return (see conditions under **Head of household** above) . **E** ____

Enter "1" if you have at least $1,500 of **child or dependent care expenses** for which you plan to claim a credit . . **F** ____

(**Note:** *Do **not** include child support payments. See **Pub. 503,** Child and Dependent Care Expenses, for details.*)

Child Tax Credit (including additional child tax credit):
- If your total income will be between $15,000 and $42,000 ($20,000 and $65,000 if married), enter "1" for each eligible child plus **1 additional**
  if you have three to five eligible children or **2 additional** if you have six or more eligible children.
- If your total income will be between $42,000 and $80,000 ($65,000 and $115,000 if married), enter "1" if you have one or two eligible children,
  "2" if you have three eligible children, "3" if you have four eligible children, or "4" if you have five or more eligible children. **G** 1

Add lines A through G and enter total here. **Note:** *This may be different from the number of exemptions you claim on your tax return.* • **H** 2

For accuracy, complete all worksheets that apply.	• If you plan to **itemize or claim adjustments to income** and want to reduce your withholding, see the **Deductions and Adjustments Worksheet** on page 2.
	• If you have **more than one job** or are **married and you and your spouse both work** and the combined earnings from all jobs exceed $35,000, see the **Two-Earner/Two-Job Worksheet** on page 2 to avoid having too little tax withheld.
	• If **neither** of the above situations applies, **stop here** and enter the number from line H on line 5 of Form W-4 below.

- - - - - Cut here and give Form W-4 to your employer. Keep the top part for your records. - - - - -

W-4	**Employee's Withholding Allowance Certificate**	OMB No. 1545-0010
rtment of the Treasury **nal Revenue Service**	• **For Privacy Act and Paperwork Reduction Act Notice, see page 2.**	2003

Type or print your first name and middle initial Iris I.	Last name Rich	**2** Your social security number 003 04 0005

Home address (number and street or rural route)
4 Everlonging Lane

3 ☐ Single ☐ Married ☐ Married, but withhold at higher Single rate.
Note: *If married, but legally separated, or spouse is a nonresident alien, check the "Single" box.*

City or town, state, and ZIP code
Emerald City, MA 00098

4 If your last name differs from that shown on your social security card, check here. You must call 1-800-772-1213 for a new card. • ☐

Total number of allowances you are claiming (from line H above **or** from the applicable worksheet on page 2)	**5**	2
Additional amount, if any, you want withheld from each paycheck	**6** $	0

I claim exemption from withholding for 2003, and I certify that I meet **both** of the following conditions for exemption:
- Last year I had a right to a refund of **all** Federal income tax withheld because I had **no** tax liability **and**
- This year I expect a refund of **all** Federal income tax withheld because I expect to have **no** tax liability.

If you meet both conditions, write "Exempt" here . . . . | **7** |

er penalties of perjury, I certify that I am entitled to the number of withholding allowances claimed on this certificate, or I am entitled to claim exempt status.

ployee's signature
m is not valid
ess you sign it.) • *Iris I. Rich* Date *June 6* 2002

Employer's name and address (Employer: Complete lines 8 and 10 only if sending to the IRS.) ouz Notpaywell, Inc. 2 Scratch Blvd., Dearth, MA 02244	**9** Office code (optional) 00	**10** Employer identification number 0998899

Cat. No. 10220Q

Rev. 12/01

Massachusetts Department of Revenue

Form TA-1
Application for Original Registration

Check As Many As Apply

1. **A** 1. ☒ Employer under the Income Tax Withholding Law (payroll tax)
  2. ☐ Withholding for Pension Plans, Annuities and Retirement Distributions

B 1. ☒ Sales/Use Tax on Goods Vendor
  2. ☐ Sales/Use Tax on Telecommunications Services Vendor
  3. ☐ Meals Tax on Food and All Beverages
  4. ☐ Purchasing in MA for Out-of-State Resale Only

C ☐ Room Occupancy Excise

Note: If you are selling cigarettes at retail, see instructions.

D ☐ Governmental or Charitable Exempt Purchaser
E ☐ Chapter 180 Organization Selling Alcoholic Beverages
F ☐ Use Tax Purchaser
G ☐ Boston Sightseeing Tour Surcharge
H ☐ Boston Vehicular Rental Transaction Surcharge
I ☐ Parking Facilities Surcharge in Boston, Springfield and/or Worcester
J ☐ Cigar and Smoking Tobacco Excise

2. Federal Identification number
0 4 5 5 5 5 5 5 5

3. Social Security number

4. No. of locations

Principal Place of Business

5. Owner, partnership or legal corporate name
E v e r e t t & L u k e ' s L e o p a r d s , I n c .
Name (cont'd.)

6. Number and street **(PO box is not acceptable)**
3 J u n g l e R o a d

7. City or town
W a y l a n d

8. State
M A

9. Zip
0 2 2 0 0 —

10. (Area code) Telephone number
(5 0 8) 5 5 5 — 1 2 1 2

General Information. If a corporation, trust, association, fiduciary, or partnership — you must complete Schedule TA-3.

11. Indicate type of organization:
☒ Corporation ☐ Trust or association ☐ Sole proprietor ☐ Fiduciary ☐ Partnership ☐ Other (specify): _____

12. Indicate type of business:
☒ Retail trade ☐ Wholesale trade ☐ Manufacturing ☐ Construction ☐ Governmental ☐ Finance ☐ Real estate ☐ Service
☐ Other (specify): _____ **13.** Describe nature of business: Cat toy sales

14. Business activity code 5 9 9 5 **15.** Check applicable box: ☒ Profit ☐ Non-profit

16. If subsidiary corporation
Name of parent corporation ►
Federal Identification number

17. If sole proprietor (sole owner)
Name of owner ►
Social Security number

18. Reason for applying:
☒ Started new business ☐ Purchased existing business — enter name, address, and Federal Identification number of previous owner
Federal Identification number

☐ Organizational change — Federal Identification number and close date of previous organization **must** be entered, or application will be returned. ☐ Other (attach explanation)
Federal Identification number

	Mo	Day	Yr
Close date:			

Background Information

19. Are any Massachusetts tax returns due or any Massachusetts taxes owed by your firm? ☐ Yes ☒ No. If yes, please explain:

20. Have you ever been issued a Certificate of Registration that was later revoked? ☐ Yes ☒ No. If yes, please explain:

Exempt Organizations

21. If you are applying for exempt purchaser status, be sure to include a copy of your IRS letter of exemption under Section 501(c)(3) of the Internal Revenue Code. Subordinate organizations covered under an IRS group exemption letter should include a copy of the group exemption ruling **and** a copy of the organization's directory page listing the organization as an approved subordinate. Both of the questions below must be answered.
A. Are you exempt from paying U.S. income taxes? ☐ Yes ☐ No. B. Are you exempt from paying local property taxes? ☐ Yes ☐ No.

Location of business

Federal Identification number _____

22. Trade name

`N/A`

Trade name (cont'd.)

23. Number and street (**PO box is not acceptable**)

`3 Jungle Road`

24. City or town

`Wayland`

25. State `MA`

26. Zip `0 2 2 0 0 —`

27. (Area code) Telephone number

`(508) 555—1212`

28. Send certificate to: ☒ Principal place of business ☐ Location of business.

29. Send tax forms to: ☒ Principal place of business ☐ Location of business ☐ Other.
If "Other," complete Schedule TA-4.

Convention Center Financing District

30. Check here if your business location is within a Convention Center Financing District: ☐ (see pages 24–26 of instructions).

31. Check here if your business location is within a hotel, motel or other lodging establishment in Boston or Cambridge: ☐

Filing Frequencies

32. Is this location seasonal? (See instructions) ☐ Yes ☒ No.
If "yes," check month(s) or partial month(s) business operates.

Check month(s)	Jan	Feb	Mar	Apr	May	Jun	Jul	Aug	Sep	Oct	Nov	Dec
Withholding												
Sales/Use on Goods												
Sales/Use on Telecom. Services												
Meals												
Room Occupancy												

33. Indicate 12-month **estimate** of tax to be withheld, collected or paid for **each** applicable tax. **Check the appropriate box(es).**

Check appropriate box	$0–$100	$101–$1,200	$1,201–$25,000	over $25,000
Withholding			X	
Check appropriate box(es)	$0–$100	$101–$1,200	over $1,200	
Sales/Use on Goods		X		
Sales/Use on Telecom. Services				
Meals				
Room Occupancy				
Use Tax Purchaser				

Tax Type Information

Withholding

34. Date you were first required to withhold taxes at this location.

Mo `07` Day `02` Yr `03`

35. Number of employees in Massachusetts: `3`

Sales/Use Tax on Goods

36. Date you were first required to collect sales/use tax at this location.

Mo `07` Day `02` Yr `02`

Sales/Use Tax on Telecommunications Services

37. Date you were first required to collect sales/use tax on telecommunications services at this location. Mo ☐ Day ☐ Yr ☐

Meals Tax on Food and All Beverages

38. Check if you serve: ☐ Food ☐ Beer ☐ Wine ☐ Alc. bev.

39. Check if food/beverage vending machine: ☐

40. Date you were first required to collect meals tax. Mo ☐ Day ☐ Yr ☐

41. Name and address on liquor license at this location.

42. Seating capacity:

Room Occupancy

43. Date you were first required to collect room occupancy tax. Mo ☐ Day ☐ Yr ☐

44. Locality code `MA`

45. Number of rooms:

Use Tax Purchaser

46. Date you were first required to pay use tax. Mo ☐ Day ☐ Yr ☐

Convention Center Financing Surcharges

47. Date you were first required to collect: a. Boston Sightseeing Tour Surcharge. Mo ☐ Day ☐ Yr ☐

b. Boston Vehicular Rental Transaction Surcharge. Mo ☐ Day ☐ Yr ☐

c. Parking Facilities Surcharge in Boston, Springfield and/or Worcester. Mo ☐ Day ☐ Yr ☐

Cigar and Smoking Tobacco Excise

48. Date you were first required to collect cigar and smoking tobacco excise. Mo ☐ Day ☐ Yr ☐

Mail to: Massachusetts Department of Revenue, Data Integration Bureau, PO Box 7022, Boston, MA 02204.

I hereby certify that the statements made herein have been examined by me and are, to the best of my knowledge and belief, true and correct. Signed under the pains and penalties of perjury. The signing of this application is evidence that you may be individually and personally responsible for any sums required to be paid to the Commonwealth, under MGL, Chapters 62B, Sec. 5; 64G, Sec. 7B; 64H, Sec. 16 and 64I, Sec. 17.

Your signature	Title	Date
Everett O'Neill	*Pres.*	*7/2/03*

form 9

200

M-942 **W42**	MASSACHUSETTS DEPARTMENT OF REVENUE

EMPLOYER'S MONTHLY RETURN OF INCOME TAXES WITHHELD

YOU MUST FILE THIS FORM EVEN THOUGH NO TAX MAY BE DUE.

FEDERAL IDENTIFICATION NUMBER	BE SURE THIS RETURN COVERS THE CORRECT PERIOD	FOR MONTH/YEAR	NUMBER OF EMPLOYEES FROM WHOM TAXES WERE WITHHELD:	3
04-5555555				

IF ANY INFOR-MATION IS INCORRECT, SEE INSTRUC-TIONS.	Everett & Luke's Catnip, Inc. 7 Huckleberry Lane Oliver, MA 99999

☐ Check here if this is a final return. ☐ Check here if EFT payment.

1.	AMOUNT WITHHELD	250.00
2.	ADJUSTMENT FOR PRIOR AMOUNT WITHHELD*	
3.	AMOUNT DUE AFTER ADJUST-MENT (NOT LESS THAN "0")	
4.	PENALTIES	
5.	INTEREST	
6.	TOTAL AMOUNT DUE (ADD LINES 3, 4 AND 5)	250.00

Return is due with payment on or before the 15th day of the month following the month indicated above, except during March, June, September and December — then due the last day of the following month. Make check payable to Commonwealth of Massachusetts. Mail to: **Massachusetts Department of Revenue, PO Box 7038, Boston, MA 02204.**

I declare under the penalties of perjury that this return (including any accompanying schedules and statements) has been examined by me and to the best of my knowledge and belief is a true, correct and complete return.

Signature *Everett O'Neill*   Title *Pres.*   Date *6/5/03*

CHECK HERE IF USING THE BACK OF THIS FORM: ☐

*Explain any adjustment on reverse or it will be disallowed.

New owners — do not use previous owner's form to file your return. Any change in ownership or organization requires a new registration. You must file a new Form TA-1.

LINE 2 ADJUSTMENT INFORMATION	AS REPORTED	CORRECTED	STATE REASON FOR ADJUSTMENT REQUEST:
AMOUNT WITHHELD			
ADJUSTMENT PRIOR PERIOD			
AMOUNT PAID			
REPORTED UNDER FED. IDENT. NO.			
REPORTING PERIOD IN ERROR			

88M 7/00 00-B02

✿ *printed on recycled paper*

form 10

**MASSACHUSETTS
DIVISION OF
EMPLOYMENT
AND TRAINING**

EMPLOYER STATUS REPORT

Complete And Return This Form Within 10 days To:
Contributions Department - Status - 5th Floor
19 Staniford Street
Boston, MA 02114-2589

PLEASE TYPE OR PRINT CLEARLY IN INK.

**ALSO COMPLETE REVERSE SIDE.
CALL (617) 626-5075 FOR ASSISTANCE.**

<table>
<tr><td colspan="5" align="center">FOR DIVISION USE ONLY</td></tr>
<tr><td colspan="2">Emp. No.:</td><td colspan="3">Subj. Date:</td></tr>
<tr><td colspan="2">Reason:</td><td>Qtr.:</td><td colspan="2">13th Wk.:</td></tr>
<tr><td colspan="2">No. Employees:</td><td>Area:</td><td colspan="2">Ind.:</td></tr>
<tr><td colspan="2">Rate Yr:</td><td>NAICS:</td><td colspan="2">Aux:</td></tr>
<tr><td colspan="3">Org.:</td><td align="center">Surcharge Yr./Rate</td><td align="center">Contribution Yr./Rate</td></tr>
<tr><td colspan="3">Deter. By:</td><td></td><td></td></tr>
<tr><td colspan="3">Pred. No.:</td><td>1.</td><td>1.</td></tr>
<tr><td colspan="3">Pred. Date:</td><td>2.</td><td>2.</td></tr>
<tr><td colspan="3">Pred. Cd.:</td><td>3.</td><td>3.</td></tr>
<tr><td colspan="3">ESR Status:</td><td>4.</td><td>4.</td></tr>
<tr><td colspan="3">Leasing Code:</td><td rowspan="2">5.</td><td rowspan="2">5.</td></tr>
<tr><td colspan="3">Employer Type:</td></tr>
</table>

Name of employing unit:
Dug's Rugs, Inc.

Trade name:
none

MA   99776

List **ALL** business locations in Massachusetts. If more than one attach a separate sheet.

13 Oriental Lane	Sherborn		
No. Street (do not use P.O. box number)	City	State	Zip Code

Mailing address: **same**

No. St./P.O. box no.	City	State	Zip Code

Address where you keep your payroll records:
same

Business phone: **508**   **555-6678**
Area Code   Number

Federal identification no.:
04-3333333

Owner, partners or officers:

Name	**S.S.A. No.**	**Home address** (do not use P.O. box numbers)	**Title**	Are officers compensated for their services?
Dug Andrews	444-55-6666	3 Edinburgh St. Portobello, MA 88993	Pres.	X Yes ☐ No
				☐ Yes ☐ No
				☐ Yes ☐ No

Type of organization: ☐ Individual   ☐ Partnership   **X** Corporation   ☐ Other (specify) _____

If corporation: date incorporated **1/6/03**   state **MA**

First date of employment in Massachusetts: **1/13/03**

Are you a client of an employee leasing company?   ☐ Yes   **X** No
If yes, name of employee leasing company _____

Are you liable for federal unemployment tax?
☐ Yes   **X** No   1st date of liability _____

Have you previously been subject to the Massachusetts Employment and Training Law?   ☐ Yes   **X** No
If yes, give account number _____ name _____

Do you hold an exemption from federal income taxes as a non-profit organization described under section 501 (c)(3) of the Internal Revenue Code?   ☐ Yes   **X** No
If Yes, please attach a copy of your exemption with this report.

Describe nature of your company's business/industry:
Oriental rug sales

Specify your principal activity. Name your principal commodity, product or service.
Oriental rug sales

If your main activity in Massachusetts is to provide support services to other locations of your company, please check appropriate box:

☐ Headquarters   ☐ Research   ☐ Warehouse
☐ Computer Center   ☐ Other (specify) _____

Did you acquire the business of a predecessor?   ☐ Yes   **X** No   If Yes, state: date acquired: _____

Name of predecessor: _____   Predecessor account number: _____

Did you acquire **ALL** or **PART** of the business of the predecessor?   ☐ ALL   ☐ PART

Acquisition of one of several locations in Massachusetts is considered **PART** of the business.

How acquired?   ☐ Purchase   ☐ Lease   ☐ Franchise   ☐ Other   (explain) _____

Did you acquire the assets of the predecessor's business?   ☐ Yes   ☐ No

Describe those assets acquired:

Describe those assets **NOT** acquired:

Will the predecessor remain in business in Massachusetts?   ☐ Yes   ☐ No   If No, give the date of last payroll: _____

If **Yes**, what is present Massachusetts location of predecessor? _____

Number of Employees: _____

No.	Street	City	State	Zip Code

Commonwealth of Massachusetts
Form 1110-A Rev. 2-00

DOMESTIC EMPLOYERS:
Did you pay $1,000 or more in cash remuneration in any calendar quarter during the current or preceding calendar year for domestic services? ☐ Yes ☐ No

AGRICULTURAL EMPLOYERS:
Did you pay $20,000 or more in cash remuneration for agricultural services during any calendar quarter of the current or preceding calendar year?
☐ Yes ☐ No

Did you employ 10 or more individuals on some day in each of 20 calendar weeks, not necessarily consecutive, in either the current or preceding calendar year? ☐ Yes ☐ No

ALL OTHER EMPLOYERS:
Did you pay wages of $1,500 or more in any calendar quarter in either the current or preceding calendar year? X Yes ☐ No

Did you employ one or more individuals on some day in each of 13 weeks, not necessarily consecutive, in either the current or preceding calendar year? X Yes ☐ No

If an "OUT OF STATE" employer, did you have a Massachusetts payroll in excess of $200? ☐ Yes ☐ No

List below the number of individuals in your employ in Massachusetts within each calendar week. Include full and part time employees, also paid officers if a corporation. An individual proprietor or a partner should not be counted as an employee. Show total Massachusetts payroll for each calendar quarter.

RECORD OF MASSACHUSETTS EMPLOYMENT IN CURRENT CALENDAR YEAR						ENTER YEAR 2003
	JANUARY	FEBRUARY	MARCH	APRIL	MAY	JUNE
Week Ending	17 24 31	7 14 21 28	7 14 21 28			
Number Employed	2 2 2	2 2 2	2 2 2			
	JULY	AUGUST	SEPTEMBER	OCTOBER	NOVEMBER	DECEMBER
Week Ending						
Number Employed						
TOTAL WAGES	1st QTR. $	2nd QTR. $	3rd QTR. $		4th QTR. $	

RECORD OF MASSACHUSETTS EMPLOYMENT IN PRECEDING CALENDAR YEAR						ENTER YEAR ____
	JANUARY	FEBRUARY	MARCH	APRIL	MAY	JUNE
Week Ending						
Number Employed						
	JULY	AUGUST	SEPTEMBER	OCTOBER	NOVEMBER	DECEMBER
Week Ending						
Number Employed						
TOTAL WAGES	1st QTR. $	2nd QTR. $	3rd QTR. $		4th QTR. $	

RECORD OF MASSACHUSETTS EMPLOYMENT IN PRECEDING CALENDAR YEAR						ENTER YEAR ____
	JANUARY	FEBRUARY	MARCH	APRIL	MAY	JUNE
Week Ending						
Number Employed						
	JULY	AUGUST	SEPTEMBER	OCTOBER	NOVEMBER	DECEMBER
Week Ending						
Number Employed						
TOTAL WAGES	1st QTR. $	2nd QTR. $	3rd QTR. $		4th QTR. $	

PREDECESSOR: I hereby certify that all information submitted by the successor is true in accordance with the transfer.

Signature: _____ Title: _____
            owner, partner or officer

THIS REPORT MUST BE SIGNED BY THE OWNER, A PARTNER OR CORPORATE OFFICER
I certify, under penalties of perjury, that all statements made hereon are true to the best of my knowledge and belief.

Name of employing unit: Dug's Rugs, Inc. Date: 3/31/03

Signature: *Dug Andrews* Title: Pres.

1110-A Rev. 2-00

REVENUE SERVICE FACT SHEET

Internet: http://www.detma.org/revenue

EMPLOYER GUIDE TO D.E.T. REVENUE SERVICES

D.E.T. Information

Address changes	(617)	626-5040
Changes in ownership/operation	(617)	626-5075
Corrections to quarterly contribution reports (Form 0001)	(617)	626-5090
Delinquent account resolution	(617)	626-5770
Federal unemployment tax (FUTA)	(617)	626-6895
Liability for contributions	(617)	626-5075
New business registration	(617)	626-5075
Refunds	(617)	626-5091
Wages subject to contributions	(617)	626-5090
Contribution rates	(617)	626-6895
Quarterly contribution reports (Form 0001)	(617)	626-5243
Unemployment Health Insurance (Collections)	(617)	626-5060

Quarterly Contribution Report (D.E.T. Form 0001)

To simplify the reporting process for employers, D.E.T. mails preprinted Forms 0001 to all active employers each quarter at least 30 days prior to the due date. If you don't receive your Form 0001, or if you need help filling it out, call 617-626-5243 or the Revenue District Office nearest you:

Greater Boston/Eastern Massachusetts	(617)	626-6815
West/Central	(413)	737-0213

Quarterly Filing and Payment

Filing your quarterly reports on time ensures that you qualify for full FUTA credit with the IRS and that your account is properly credited before your new annual rate is set. You avoid late-filer penalties and interest charges if you file promptly.

Change of Address

If your business is changing location, or if you want D.E.T. to send benefit charges or wage information requests to another address, simply fill out the appropriate section of the Employer Data Change Form (Form 1897) enclosed with the Form 0001. We'll make the change when we process your quarterly report.

Suspension of Accounts

If your business has ceased operating or you do not expect to have employees next year, D.E.T. will suspend your account and stop sending you quarterly contribution reports (Form 0001). Call a Revenue District Office or 617-626-5075 and request an Application to Suspend (Form 0740).

Publications

If you'd like to know more about the unemployment insurance system and how you can lower the costs to your firm, we'll send you easy-to-read publications written especially for employers. Call 617-626-5075 for your free copy of either publication.

- Simplifying the Employment and Training Law - A Guide for Employers
- How Experience Rating Works

Forms and publications mentioned, except Form 1897, above can be downloaded from the Internet.

Commonwealth of Massachusetts
P-1919 R1-99

☒ **NEW FILING**
☐ **RENEWAL**

BUSINESS CERTIFICATE
City of Boston

This Certificate Expires: _____

Under the provisions of Chapter One Hundred Ten, Section Five of the General Laws, as amended, the undersigned hereby declares that a business under the title of:

Luke's Baritone Horns
_____
(please print)

is being conducted at: _____

123 Elm Street,   Boston, MA   12345
_____
                                            ZIP CODE

BY THE FOLLOWING-NAMED
PERSONS OR CORPORATION:

FULL NAME	CORPORATION OR RESIDENCE ADDRESS
Luke O'Neill	123 Elm St., Boston, MA 12345

SIGNED: *Luke O'Neill*

IMPORTANT NOTICE: This Certificate expires four years from the date of issue. If you cease conducting business before that time, the law requires that you contact the City Clerk and withdraw this Certificate.

Contact Telephone Number: 508-555-1212   Type of Business Instrument Sales

THE COMMONWEALTH OF MASSACHUSETTS

Suffolk: ss.   Date: October 31, 2003

Personally appeared before me, the above-named Luke O'Neill

On this date and made oath that the foregoing statement is true.

Mickey Bengal

CH. 227, sec. 5A ☐   Justice of the Peace
Seal   Notary Public
                            My commission expires: 11 / 1 / 05

X-6422   **Non-residents: Please see reverse side.**

CERTIFICATE AND STATEMENT

(for Non-residents doing business in Massachusetts)

Filing Fee: $25.00 (in addition to regular fee)

Pursuant of MGL Ch. 227, sec. 5A, I/We hereby appoint the City Clerk of the City of Boston, and his successors in office, as my/our true and lawful agent upon whom all lawful process may be served in any action arising out of the business described on the front hereof.

Signature(s): *Luke O'Neill*

SAMPLE FORM W-2: WAGE AND TAX STATEMENT

Control number	.....	Void ☐	For Official Use Only · OMB No. 1545-0008

Employer identification number	1 Wages, tips, other compensation	2 Federal income tax withheld
04-8884444	$ 25,650.00	$ 5,050.00

Employer's name, address, and ZIP code

Chef of the Future, Inc.

80 7th Ave.

Brookline, MA 44444

3 Social security wages	4 Social security tax withheld
$ 25,650.00	$ 1,590.30

5 Medicare wages and tips	6 Medicare tax withheld
$ 25,650.00	$ 371.93

7 Social security tips	8 Allocated tips
$ 0	$ 0

Employee's social security number

123-44-5566

9 Advance EIC payment	10 Dependent care benefits
$ 0	$ 0

Employee's first name and initial   Last name

Jackie N. Norton

3 Amersterdam Ave.

Brookline, MA 44444

11 Nonqualified plans	12a See instructions for box 12
$ 0	Code $ 0

13 Statutory employee ☐ Retirement plan ☐ Third-party sick pay ☐	12b Code $
14 Other	12c Code $
	12d Code $

Employee's address and ZIP code

State	Employer's state ID number	16 State wages, tips, etc.	17 State income tax	18 Local wages, tips, etc.	19 Local income tax	20 Locality name
	44488778	$ 26,650.00	$ 565.00	$	$	
		$	$	$	$	

W-2 **Wage and Tax Statement** (99)

● ● ● ●

(Rev. February 2002)

Cat. No. 10134D

Department of the Treasury—Internal Revenue Service

For Privacy Act and Paperwork Reduction Act Notice, see separate instructions.

A For Social Security Administration—Send this entire with Form W-3 to the Social Security Administration; copies are **not** acceptable.

Do Not Cut, Fold, or Staple Forms on This Page — Do Not Cut, Fold, or Staple Forms on This Page

SAMPLE FORMS 1099 AND 1096: MISCELLANEOUS INCOME

9595 ☐ VOID ☐ CORRECTED

PAYER'S name, street address, city, state, ZIP code, and telephone no.	**1** Rents	OMB No. 1545-0115	
Jeremy Michaels XYZ Builders 123 Maple Avenue Oaktown, VA 22000 703-123-4567	$ **2** Royalties $	20**02** Form **1099-MISC**	**Miscellaneous Income**

		3 Other income $	**4** Federal income tax withheld $	**Copy A** **For**
PAYER'S Federal identification number 10-9999999	RECIPIENT'S identification number 123-45-6789	**5** Fishing boat proceeds $	**6** Medical and health care payments $	**Internal Revenue Service Center** File with Form 1096.

RECIPIENT'S name

Zachary Austin
Rock Hill Drywall

7 Nonemployee compensation
$ 5500.00

8 Substitute payments in lieu of dividends or interest
$

For Privacy Act and Paperwork Reduction Act Notice, see the **2002 General Instructions for Forms 1099, 1098, 5498, and W-2G.**

Street address (including apt. no.)

456 Flower Lane

9 Payer made direct sales of $5,000 or more of consumer products to a buyer (recipient) for resale ▶ ☐

10 Crop insurance proceeds
$

City, state, and ZIP code
Oaktown, VA 22000

11

12

Account number (optional)

2nd TIN not. ☐

13 Excess golden parachute payments
$

14 Gross proceeds paid to an attorney
$

15

16 State tax withheld
$
$

17 State/Payer's state no.

18 State income
$
$

Form **1099-MISC**

Cat. No. 14425J

Department of the Treasury - Internal Revenue Service

Do Not Staple   6969

Form **1096** Department of the Treasury Internal Revenue Service	**Annual Summary and Transmittal of U.S. Information Returns**	OMB No. 1545-0108 20**02**

FILER'S name

Everett's Rockin' CDs, Inc.

Street address (including room or suite number)

10 Simba Lane

City, state, and ZIP code
Boston, MA 03333

Name of person to contact Everett L. Lester	Telephone number (508) 555-1212	**For Official Use Only**
Fax number (508) 555-1313	E-mail address	☐☐☐☐☐☐ ☐☐

1 Employer identification number 04-2222222	**2** Social security number	**3** Total number of forms 3	**4** Federal income tax withheld $ 0	**5** Total amount reported with this Form 1096 $ $15,000

Enter an "X" in only one box below to indicate the type of form being filed.   If this is your **final return**, enter an "X" here .   .   .   ▶ ☒

W-2G 32	1098 81	1098-E 84	1098-T 83	1099-A 80	1099-B 79	1099-C 85	1099-DIV 91	1099-G 86	1099-INT 92	1099-LTC 93	1099-MISC 95	1099-MSA 94	1099-OID 96
☐	☐	☐	☐	☐	☐	☐	☐	☐	☐	☐	☒	☐	☐

1099-PATR 97	1099-Q 31	1099-R 98	1099-S 75	5498 28	5498-MSA 27
☐	☐	☐	☐	☐	☐

SAMPLE FORM 8109-B: FEDERAL TAX DEPOSIT COUPONS

AMOUNT OF DEPOSIT (Do NOT type, please print.)

DOLLARS | CENTS

TAX YEAR MONTH →

EMPLOYER IDENTIFICATION NUMBER →

BANK NAME/ DATE STAMP

Name _____

Address _____

City _____

State _____ ZIP _____

IRS USE ONLY

Darken only one TYPE OF TAX		a n d	Darken only one TAX PERIOD
941	945		1st Quarter
990-C	1120		2nd Quarter
943	990-T		3rd Quarter
720	990-PF		4th Quarter
CT-1	1042		
940			35

Telephone number ( )

FOR BANK USE IN MICR ENCODING

Federal Tax Deposit Coupon
Form 8109-B (Rev. 4-96)

SAMPLE FORM 1040-ES: ESTIMATED TAX PAYMENT VOUCHER

Form **1040-ES**
Department of the Treasury
Internal Revenue Service

2002 Payment Voucher **3**

OMB No. 1545-0087

File only if you are making a payment of estimated tax by check or money order. Mail this voucher with your check or money order payable to the "**United States Treasury.**" Write your social security number and "2002 Form 1040-ES" on your check or money order. Do not send cash. Enclose, but do not staple or attach, your payment with this voucher.

Calendar year- Due Sept. 16, 2002

Amount of estimated tax you are paying by check or money order.

Dollars	Cents
3,000	00

Type or print

Your first name and initial	Your last name	Your social security number
Huckle D.	Katt	114–55–6666

If joint payment, complete for spouse

Spouse's first name and initial	Spouse's last name	Spouse's social security number

Address (number, street, and apt. no.)
4 Island Rd.

City, state, and ZIP code (If a foreign address, enter city, province or state, postal code, and country.)
Holliston, MA 01746

For Privacy Act and Paperwork Reduction Act Notice, see instructions on page 5.

INDEX

O

Occupational Safety and Health Administration (OSHA), 69, 70, 177, 178
    poster, 70
    publications, 70
    regulations, 69
overtime, 92

P

partners, 9, 10
partnership, 9, 13, 18, 27
    advantages, 9
    characteristics, 9
    disadvantages, 10
patent, 125, 126, 127
payment, 117
    cash, 117
    checks, 118
        refunds, 118
    credit card, 118, 119
    money orders, 117
    travelers' checks, 117
pension plans. *See retirement accounts*
personnel records, 104
pierce the corporate veil, 14, 18
polygraph test, 78
posters, 103
professional corporation, 12, 29. *See also corporation*
profits, 35, 159
property, 18, 43–49
    buying, 47–48
    leasing, 45, 46, 45–47
    zoning, 45, 48, 51
proprietorship, 9, 18, 66, 160
    advantages, 9
    characteristics, 9
    disadvantages, 9
publicity, 3, 25
Pure Food and Drug Act of 1906, 71

R

real estate. *See property*
Regulation Z, 120, 121
retail site, 44
retirement accounts, 36
retirement plans, 96, 162
Robinson-Patman Act of 1936, 124
Roth IRA, 95

S

S corporation, 11, 12, 13, 14, 15, 16, 17, 159, 161, 164, 171
savings, 36
search engines, 149, 149–150
Secretary of State, 18, 25, 28, 30
securities, 40
service mark, 30, 126
sexual harassment, 81, 88, 89, 88–91
    federal law, 88
    Massachusetts law, 90
    protection against, 90
shareholders, 10, 11, 163
Sherman Antitrust Act of 1890, 124
sick days, 95
signs, 45, 48
Small Business Administration, 5, 38
    loans, 38
Small Necessities Leave Act, 97
smoking, 74, 75
    Massachusetts law, 74
Social Security, 165
spamming, 151
start-up procedures, 18
state laws, 129
state tax, 169
    corporate income tax, 171
    exemptions, 169, 170
    meal tax, 169
    out of state, 170
    room occupancy tax, 171
    sales, 169, 170
    tax number, 170
    tobacco tax, 171
    unemployment compensation taxes, 171
    withholding, 170
stock, 18, 39, 40, 162
sublease, 47

SPHINX® PUBLISHING ORDER FORM

BILL TO:		SHIP TO:	
Phone #	Terms	F.O.B. Chicago, IL	Ship Date

Charge my: ☐ VISA   ☐ MasterCard   ☐ American Express

☐ **Money Order or Personal Check**

Credit Card Number   Expiration Date

Qty	ISBN	Title	Retail	Ext.
		SPHINX PUBLISHING NATIONAL TITLES		
	1-57248-148-X	Cómo Hacer su Propio Testamento	$16.95	
	1-57248-226-5	Cómo Restablecer su propio Crédito y Renegociar sus Deudas	$21.95	
	1-57248-147-1	Cómo Solicitar su Propio Divorcio	$24.95	
	1-57248-238-9	The 529 College Savings Plan	$16.95	
	1-57248-166-8	The Complete Book of Corporate Forms	$24.95	
	1-57248-229-X	The Complete Legal Guide to Senior Care	$21.95	
	1-57248-201-X	The Complete Patent Book	$26.95	
	1-57248-163-3	Crime Victim's Guide to Justice (2E)	$21.95	
	1-57248-251-6	The Entrepreneur's Internet Handbook	$21.95	
	1-57248-159-5	Essential Guide to Real Estate Contracts	$18.95	
	1-57248-160-9	Essential Guide to Real Estate Leases	$18.95	
	1-57248-254-0	Family Limited Partnership	$26.95	
	1-57248-139-0	Grandparents' Rights (3E)	$24.95	
	1-57248-188-9	Guía de Inmigración a Estados Unidos (3E)	$24.95	
	1-57248-187-0	Guía de Justicia para Víctimas del Crimen	$21.95	
	1-57248-103-X	Help Your Lawyer Win Your Case (2E)	$14.95	
	1-57248-164-1	How to Buy a Condominium or Townhome (2E)	$19.95	
	1-57248-191-9	How to File Your Own Bankruptcy (5E)	$21.95	
	1-57248-132-3	How to File Your Own Divorce (4E)	$24.95	
	1-57248-083-1	How to Form a Limited Liability Company	$22.95	
	1-57248-231-1	How to Form a Nonprofit Corporation (2E)	$24.95	
	1-57248-133-1	How to Form Your Own Corporation (3E)	$24.95	
	1-57248-224-9	How to Form Your Own Partnership (2E)	$24.95	
	1-57248-232-X	How to Make Your Own Simple Will (3E)	$18.95	
	1-57248-200-1	How to Register Your Own Copyright (4E)	$24.95	
	1-57248-104-8	How to Register Your Own Trademark (3E)	$21.95	
	1-57248-233-8	How to Write Your Own Living Will (3E)	$18.95	
	1-57248-156-0	How to Write Your Own Premarital Agreement (3E)	$24.95	
	1-57248-230-3	Incorporate in Delaware from Any State	$24.95	
	1-57248-158-7	Incorporate in Nevada from Any State	$24.95	
	1-57248-250-8	Inmigración a los EE.UU. Paso a Paso	$22.95	
	1-57071-333-2	Jurors' Rights (2E)	$12.95	
	1-57248-223-0	Legal Research Made Easy (3E)	$21.95	
	1-57248-165-X	Living Trusts and Other Ways to Avoid Probate (3E)	$24.95	
	1-57248-186-2	Manual de Beneficios para el Seguro Social	$18.95	
	1-57248-220-6	Mastering the MBE	$16.95	
	1-57248-167-6	Most Valuable Bus. Legal Forms You'll Ever Need (3E)	$21.95	
	1-57248-130-7	Most Valuable Personal Legal Forms You'll Ever Need	$24.95	
	1-57248-098-X	The Nanny and Domestic Help Legal Kit	$22.95	
	1-57248-089-0	Neighbor v. Neighbor (2E)	$16.95	
	1-57248-169-2	The Power of Attorney Handbook (4E)	$19.95	
	1-57248-149-8	Repair Your Own Credit and Deal with Debt	$18.95	
	1-57248-217-6	Sexual Harassment: Your Guide to Legal Action	$18.95	
	1-57248-219-2	The Small Business Owner's Guide to Bankruptcy	$21.95	
	1-57248-168-4	The Social Security Benefits Handbook (3E)	$18.95	
	1-57248-216-8	Social Security Q&A	$12.95	
	1-57248-221-4	Teen Rights	$22.95	
	1-57248-236-2	Unmarried Parents' Rights (2E)	$19.95	
	1-57248-161-7	U.S.A. Immigration Guide (4E)	$24.95	
	1-57248-192-7	The Visitation Handbook	$18.95	
	1-57248-225-7	Win Your Unemployment Compensation Claim (2E)	$21.95	
	1-57248-138-2	Winning Your Personal Injury Claim (2E)	$24.95	
	1-57248-162-5	Your Right to Child Custody, Visitation and Support (2E)	$24.95	
	1-57248-157-9	Your Rights When You Owe Too Much	$16.95	
		CALIFORNIA TITLES		
	1-57248-150-1	CA Power of Attorney Handbook (2E)	$18.95	
	1-57248-151-X	How to File for Divorce in CA (3E)	$26.95	
	1-57071-356-1	How to Make a CA Will	$16.95	
	1-57248-145-5	How to Probate and Settle an Estate in California	$26.95	
	1-57248-146-3	How to Start a Business in CA	$18.95	
	1-57248-194-3	How to Win in Small Claims Court in CA (2E)	$18.95	
	1-57248-196-X	The Landlord's Legal Guide in CA	$24.95	
		FLORIDA TITLES		
	1-57071-363-4	Florida Power of Attorney Handbook (2E)	$16.95	
	1-57248-176-5	How to File for Divorce in FL (7E)	$26.95	
	1-57248-177-3	How to Form a Corporation in FL (5E)	$24.95	
	1-57248-203-6	How to Form a Limited Liability Co. in FL (2E)	$24.95	
	1-57071-401-0	How to Form a Partnership in FL	$22.95	

Form Continued on Following Page   **SUBTOTAL**

To order, call Sourcebooks at 1-800-432-7444 or FAX (630) 961-2168 (Bookstores, libraries, wholesalers—please call for discount)
Prices are subject to change without notice.
Find more legal information at: www.SphinxLegal.com

SPHINX® PUBLISHING ORDER FORM

Qty	ISBN	Title	Retail	Ext.
_____	1-57248-113-7	How to Make a FL Will (6E)	$16.95	_____
_____	1-57248-088-2	How to Modify Your FL Divorce Judgment (4E)	$24.95	_____
_____	1-57248-144-7	How to Probate and Settle an Estate in FL (4E)	$26.95	_____
_____	1-57248-081-5	How to Start a Business in FL (5E)	$16.95	_____
_____	1-57248-204-4	How to Win in Small Claims Court in FL (7E)	$18.95	_____
_____	1-57248-202-8	Land Trusts in Florida (6E)	$29.95	_____
_____	1-57248-123-4	Landlords' Rights and Duties in FL (8E)	$21.95	_____

GEORGIA TITLES

Qty	ISBN	Title	Retail	Ext.
_____	1-57248-137-4	How to File for Divorce in GA (4E)	$21.95	_____
_____	1-57248-180-3	How to Make a GA Will (4E)	$21.95	_____
_____	1-57248-140-4	How to Start a Business in Georgia (2E)	$16.95	_____

ILLINOIS TITLES

Qty	ISBN	Title	Retail	Ext.
_____	1-57248-244-3	Child Custody, Visitation, and Support in IL	$24.95	_____
_____	1-57248-206-0	How to File for Divorce in IL (3E)	$24.95	_____
_____	1-57248-170-6	How to Make an IL Will (3E)	$16.95	_____
_____	1-57248-247-8	How to Start a Business in IL (3E)	$21.95	_____
_____	1-57248-252-4	The Landlord's Legal Guide in IL	$24.95	_____

MASSACHUSETTS TITLES

Qty	ISBN	Title	Retail	Ext.
_____	1-57248-128-5	How to File for Divorce in MA (3E)	$24.95	_____
_____	1-57248-115-3	How to Form a Corporation in MA	$24.95	_____
_____	1-57248-108-0	How to Make a MA Will (2E)	$16.95	_____
_____	1-57248-248-6	How to Start a Business in MA (3E)	$21.95	_____
_____	1-57248-209-5	The Landlord's Legal Guide in MA	$24.95	_____

MICHIGAN TITLES

Qty	ISBN	Title	Retail	Ext.
_____	1-57248-215-X	How to File for Divorce in MI (3E)	$24.95	_____
_____	1-57248-182-X	How to Make a MI Will (3E)	$16.95	_____
_____	1-57248-183-8	How to Start a Business in MI (3E)	$18.95	_____

MINNESOTA TITLES

Qty	ISBN	Title	Retail	Ext.
_____	1-57248-142-0	How to File for Divorce in MN	$21.95	_____
_____	1-57248-179-X	How to Form a Corporation in MN	$24.95	_____
_____	1-57248-178-1	How to Make a MN Will (2E)	$16.95	_____

NEW YORK TITLES

Qty	ISBN	Title	Retail	Ext.
_____	1-57248-193-5	Child Custody, Visitation and Support in NY	$26.95	_____
_____	1-57248-141-2	How to File for Divorce in NY (2E)	$26.95	_____
_____	1-57248-249-4	How to Form a Corporation in NY (2E)	$24.95	_____
_____	1-57248-095-5	How to Make a NY Will (2E)	$16.95	_____
_____	1-57248-199-4	How to Start a Business in NY (2E)	$18.95	_____

Qty	ISBN	Title	Retail	Ext.
_____	1-57248-198-6	How to Win in Small Claims Court in NY (2E)	$18.95	_____
_____	1-57248-197-8	Landlords' Legal Guide in NY	$24.95	_____
_____	1-57071-188-7	New York Power of Attorney Handbook	$19.95	_____
_____	1-57248-122-6	Tenants' Rights in NY	$21.95	_____

NEW JERSEY TITLES

Qty	ISBN	Title	Retail	Ext.
_____	1-57248-239-7	How to File for Divorce in NJ	$24.95	_____

NORTH CAROLINA TITLES

Qty	ISBN	Title	Retail	Ext.
_____	1-57248-185-4	How to File for Divorce in NC (3E)	$22.95	_____
_____	1-57248-129-3	How to Make a NC Will (3E)	$16.95	_____
_____	1-57248-184-6	How to Start a Business in NC (3E)	$18.95	_____
_____	1-57248-091-2	Landlords' Rights & Duties in NC	$21.95	_____

OHIO TITLES

Qty	ISBN	Title	Retail	Ext.
_____	1-57248-190-0	How to File for Divorce in OH (2E)	$24.95	_____
_____	1-57248-174-9	How to Form a Corporation in OH	$24.95	_____
_____	1-57248-173-0	How to Make an OH Will	$16.95	_____

PENNSYLVANIA TITLES

Qty	ISBN	Title	Retail	Ext.
_____	1-57248-242-7	Child Custody, Visitation and Support in Pennsylvania	$26.95	_____
_____	1-57248-211-7	How to File for Divorce in PA (3E)	$26.95	_____
_____	1-57248-094-7	How to Make a PA Will (2E)	$16.95	_____
_____	1-57248-112-9	How to Start a Business in PA (2E)	$18.95	_____
_____	1-57248-245-1	The Landlord's Legal Guide in PA	$24.95	_____

TEXAS TITLES

Qty	ISBN	Title	Retail	Ext.
_____	1-57248-171-4	Child Custody, Visitation, and Support in TX	$22.95	_____
_____	1-57248-172-2	How to File for Divorce in TX (3E)	$24.95	_____
_____	1-57248-114-5	How to Form a Corporation in TX (2E)	$24.95	_____
_____	1-57248-255-9	How to Make a TX Will (3E)	$16.95	_____
_____	1-57248-214-1	How to Probate and Settle an Estate in TX (3E)	$26.95	_____
_____	1-57248-228-1	How to Start a Business in TX (3E)	$18.95	_____
_____	1-57248-111-0	How to Win in Small Claims Court in TX (2E)	$16.95	_____
_____	1-57248-110-2	Landlords' Rights and Duties in TX (2E)	$21.95	_____

SUBTOTAL THIS PAGE _____

SUBTOTAL PREVIOUS PAGE _____

Shipping — $5.00 for 1st book, $1.00 each additional _____

Illinois residents add 6.75% sales tax _____

Connecticut residents add 6.00% sales tax _____

TOTAL _____

To order, call Sourcebooks at 1-800-432-7444 or FAX (630) 961-2168 (Bookstores, libraries, wholesalers—please call for discount)
Prices are subject to change without notice.
Find more legal information at: **www.SphinxLegal.com**